Using excellent resources from Christian thinkers and marketplace leaders, the authors have contributed an approach to theological reflection that takes this hidden gem of education out of unconscious preoccupation and into intentional habit. Their model is very useful and applicable across cultures for many reasons, especially for its emphasis on the community's participation in one's growth in self- and God-awareness. I recommend this hope-inspiring guide to everyone engaged in theological training and continuing education.

—**CHOON SAM FONG**, academic dean, Baptist Theological Seminary, Singapore

Jim Wilson and Earl Waggoner have written an important and helpful book for pastors engaged in the practice of ministry. Ministry flows from the inside out. Pastors need to attend to their interior life in order to serve in ways that are obedient and faithful. The authors invite ministry leaders to pause in the middle of their work to focus on deeper theological reflection so that in greater ways they might live into matters of character and abiding in Christ. I highly recommend this book to you.

—**KURT N. FREDRICKSON**, associate dean for doctor of ministry studies, associate professor of pastoral ministry, Fuller Theological Seminary

Theological reflection is an essential skill for ministry leaders, yet many have never learned how to do it well. Leaders think about theology and ministry but lack a model for flowing those two streams together in meaningful ways. The men who wrote this book model this process, have coached hundreds of emerging leaders on developing these skills, and now have produced this helpful guide to teaching others how to do it. Theology must inform practice. The insights you are about to read outline a workable process to make that happen.

—**JEFF IORG**, president, Gateway Seminary

In a culture defined by hurry, *A Guide to Theological Reflection* asks busy pastors, leaders, and ministry students to do the unthinkable—to pause and reflect on how our beliefs translate into our ministry. With seasoned wisdom, accessible style, and practical tools, this volume helpfully coaches us on the who, what, when, where, why, and how of this crucial reflection.

—**CHRIS MORGAN**, dean and professor of theology, School of Christian Ministries, California Baptist University

It's tempting to assume that doing theology means getting your doctrine right with ever-increasing levels of precision. That might be okay for students in a systematic theology class, but it's a bad assumption for those ministering to real people. As Jesus showed us with people as diverse as the rich young ruler, the tax collector Zacchaeus, and the woman at the well, he didn't lecture them on doctrine; his theology was embodied in the way he treated them. Those of us seeking to proclaim and exemplify good theology in ministry situations can learn a lot from Jim Wilson and Earl Waggoner's book. *A Guide to Theological Reflection* is the GPS for getting from doctrine to redemptive ministerial practice.

—**MARSHALL SHELLEY,** director of the doctor
of ministry program, Denver Seminary

Wilson and Waggoner have pulled theological reflection off the dusty seminary shelf and breathed it full of new life. They offer specific hands-on tools for reflection during that much-needed "pause"—the space before we act in specific ministry situations. This is a thorough yet practical work, bringing theological reflection directly to bear on ministry practice. It's a vital resource for mentors, seasoned leaders, and rookies in ministry. Plus, the excellent bibliography is worth the cost of the book.

—**DARYL L. SMITH,** associate professor
emeritus of mentoring and leadership,
Asbury Theological Seminary

Socrates was reputed to have said, "An unexamined life is not worth living." The contention of this book is that an unexamined ministry is just plain dangerous. The authors then makes several radical but important claims, such as that ministry leaders need more theological reflection, not less; that our ministry action should grow from our theology; and that Scripture should be our first and primary source for such reflection. This book recommends useful tools to help us pause from our incessant ministry activity to reflect on what and how we are doing and if we are pursuing ministry success as God sees it.

—**DONALD W. SWEETING,** president,
Colorado Christian University

A GUIDE TO
THEOLOGICAL
REFLECTION

A GUIDE TO

THEOLOGICAL

REFLECTION

A Fresh Approach for Practical Ministry Courses and Theological Field Education

Jim L. Wilson and Earl Waggoner

ZONDERVAN ACADEMIC

ZONDERVAN ACADEMIC

A Guide to Theological Reflection
Copyright © 2020 by Jim L. Wilson and Earl Waggoner

ISBN 978-0-310-09393-0 (softcover)

ISBN 978-0-310-09394-7 (ebook)

Requests for information should be addressed to:
Zondervan, *3900 Sparks Dr. SE, Grand Rapids, Michigan 49546*

All Scripture quotations, unless otherwise indicated, are taken from The Holy Bible, New International Version®, NIV®. Copyright © 1973, 1978, 1984, 2011 by Biblica, Inc.® Used by permission of Zondervan. All rights reserved worldwide. www.Zondervan.com. The "NIV" and "New International Version" are trademarks registered in the United States Patent and Trademark Office by Biblica, Inc.®

Scripture quotations marked ESV are taken from the ESV® Bible (The Holy Bible, English Standard Version®). Copyright © 2001 by Crossway, a publishing ministry of Good News Publishers. Used by permission. All rights reserved.

Scripture quotations marked KJV are taken from the King James Version. Public domain.

Any internet addresses (websites, blogs, etc.) and telephone numbers in this book are offered as a resource. They are not intended in any way to be or imply an endorsement by Zondervan, nor does Zondervan vouch for the content of these sites and numbers for the life of this book.

No part of this publication may be reproduced, stored in a retrieval system, or transmitted in any form or by any means—electronic, mechanical, photocopy, recording, or any other—except for brief quotations in printed reviews, without the prior permission of the publisher.

Cover design and artwork: Emily Weigel
Interior design: Kait Lamphere

Printed in the United States of America

19 20 21 22 23 24 25 26 27 28 /LSC/ 15 14 13 12 11 10 9 8 7 6 5 4 3 2 1

DEDICATION

To our supportive wives
Proverbs 18:22

To my wife, Kris—dearest love and greatest encourager
—Earl Waggoner

To my wife, Susan, my best friend and ministry partner
—Jim L. Wilson

CONTENTS

ACKNOWLEDGMENTS

RESEARCH TEAM

We wish to acknowledge our coworkers on this project, Mark Bradley and Glenn Prescott, who served as the research team for the book. They produced the first drafts of some of the book, and helped with the refinement of the rest of the book.

Dr. Bradley is a New Testament scholar with rich pastoral ministry experience and currently serves as associate professor of leadership and director of Gateway Seminary's Pacific Northwest campus.

Dr. Prescott is an applied theologian with extensive experience in missions, administration, and pastoral ministry and currently serves as professor of ministry leadership, chair of the Leadership Formation Department, and director of theological field education at Gateway Seminary.

While their names are not on the cover, their influence is on every page.

MINISTRY ARTIFACTS AND REFLECTION CONTRIBUTORS

We are grateful to the following colleagues, graduates, and DMin candidates from Gateway Seminary who provided ministry artifacts, reflections, or other material for inclusion in the book. Their contributions provided real-life samples and observations.

Dr. Al Barrera
Dr. Bryan Catherman
Dr. Hubert Chau
Dr. Mike Clements

Dr. Greg Cole
Dr. James Daily
Dr. Michael Duke
Dr. Zach Edwards

Dr. Bryan Gill

Dr. Ev Hardee

Dr. John Kamiya

Dr. Steve Lennertz

Dr. Carney Lucas

Dr. Steve Long

Dr. Sean-David McGoran

Dr. Scott Payne

Dr. Jon Pennington

Dr. Ed Pincusoff

Dr. JT Reed

Chaplain Ronald Rinaldi

Rev. Mark Schweitzer

Dr. Jim Stansberry

Dr. Kevin Trick

Dr. Les Wesley

EXTERNAL PEER REVIEWERS

We are grateful to our colleagues from other educational institutions who read the penultimate draft of the manuscript and offered corrections, advice, and suggestions for how to improve the manuscript before we submitted it to the publisher.

Dr. Kurt Fredrickson, associate professor of pastoral ministry and associate dean for the doctor of ministry and continuing education at Fuller Theological Seminary

Dr. Marshall Shelley, associate professor of pastoral leadership and ministry and doctor of ministry director at Denver Seminary

Dr. Daryl Smith, retired professor of mentoring and leadership from Asbury Theological Seminary

Dr. John Swope, director of field education, assistant professor of practical theology at Ashland Theological Seminary

STUDENT READERS

We are thankful for our trusted students who read and gave us comments on how to improve the manuscript. They made significant contributions with their feedback.

Benjamin Fox, Gateway Seminary

Paul Nacin, Colorado Christian University

Patricia Neilsen, Colorado Christian University

THE THEOLOGICAL

REFLECTION

PROCESS

CHAPTER 1

THE NEED FOR THEOLOGICAL REFLECTION

At a Glance

- The biblical record is clear: ministers must "do" what they "know."
- Moses was successful at meeting the children of Israel's needs at Meribah but failed to please God because he was not fully obedient.
- A pause from doing is required to align actions with beliefs.

Sitting in the classroom, I (Wilson) struggled to listen as my theology professor taught on election and the differences between supralapsarianism and infralapsarianism. The subject was not the problem. I found theological discussion stimulating. The problem was that my body was in the seminary classroom, but my mind was back home with the church—really with one family in the church, a family whose loved one I would bury later in the week.

I did not consider myself a student-pastor. I was a pastor, who happened to be a student. On Monday mornings, before sunrise, I commuted in Southern California traffic, took classes all day long, and arrived home to catch a few hours of sleep early the next morning.

For me, seminary was not education for future ministry possibilities. I was knee-deep in ministry already. My classes were *just-in-time information* while I served on the front lines. I needed help with knowing how to minister to the people I served in an effective and theologically responsible way. I needed theology to be more than ideas and discussions.

Even with my degrees hanging on the wall and several years of pastoral experience under my belt, I (Waggoner) was not fully prepared for a new, larger pastorate. Things were radically different, and my old ways of operating did not seem relevant in this urban, culturally diverse location. How do I help a struggling couple salvage their marriage? And the conflict—how do I minister with all this conflict going on? All around me were people who were hurting, people who needed a word of hope. How could our church help?

We both wish we had had an instruction manual for these situations. We wanted a resource, a how-to book or a paint-by-numbers canvas. What we both needed was a way to convert our theology into ministry practice. We needed a bridge between the classroom and the ministry field. We needed theological reflection.

This book is intended to provide that guide for students and ministers, readers like yourself, introducing you to effective, transformative theological reflection.

A FRESH APPROACH

Often theological reflection is promoted as a way to apply theological truth to Christian practice. That is the emphasis of the "doing theology" approach,[1] which seeks to "create and nurture church members," "build and sustain the community of faith," and "communicate the faith to a wider culture."[2] This approach promotes reflection as a guidance system for theologically consistent behavior for individual believers and their faith communities. In this approach action is the chief driver in being Christian. The defining action improves understanding: doing produces knowing, in that order.[3] In short, the "doing theology" approach harnesses theological truth to aid believers in living the Christian life well.

In contrast, our approach to theological reflection is grounded in the specific practice of ministry. While "doing theology" obviously implies certain ministry practices, those practices are understood from a macro

---

1. Trevor Hart, *Faith Thinking: The Dynamics of Christian Theology* (Eugene, OR: Wipf & Stock, 1995), 189.

2. Elaine Graham, Heather Walton, and Frances Ward, *Theological Reflection: Methods* (London: SCM, 2005), 10–11.

3. Graham, Walton, and Ward, *Theological Reflection*, 188ff.

perspective—ministry practices which guide the church long-term and toward a preferred end. Our approach is more of a micro perspective concerned with using theological reflection to determine the appropriate responses to specific ministry situations. Ministers are to apply their theology to their ministry practice.

James 1:22–25 applies to ministers as well as other members of the faith community. Ministers are to be "doing" the Word in their ministry practice. They should not be guilty of "hearing only." It is possible for ministers to become biblical theoreticians, reading the Word but not doing it, being familiar with the text but not employing it, receiving God's Word and not sharing it, paralyzed in a fog of selfishness, fear, or apathy. Theological reflection requires engaging the Bible, as well as other sources, to learn how to minister to other people and then ministering to meet their needs. "But whoever looks intently into the perfect law that gives freedom, and continues in it—not forgetting what they have heard, but doing it—they will be blessed in what they do" (James 1:25).

Since the mid-1970s theological reflection has been a critical component of theological curricula of Association of Theological Schools (ATS) member schools. The essence and importance of the practice is the creation of "an explicit connection between the information being provided in the classroom and the practice of ministry in the field."[4] As an integrative tool, theological reflection attempts to bring together biblical, historical, doctrinal, and practical data with the real-world practice of ministry, all through a reflective process. It builds a bridge between lofty theological ideas and the application of those ideas in the real world. Our approach serves that end, using theological reflection as a way of informing ministry practice.

Some of the elements of this book are meant specifically for use in college and seminary classrooms. However, most features will prove helpful in the parish, on the mission field, or in any ministry setting. For example, how to journal well (chap. 5) is a skill that will serve ministers in their formative years in the classroom and throughout their ministries.

---

4. Edward Foley, "Reflective Believing: Reimagining Theological Reflection in an Age of Diversity," *Reflective Practice: Formation and Supervision in Ministry* 34 (2014): 61, http://journals.sfu.ca/rpfs/index.php/rpfs/article/view/325/319. Foley offers a brief but good history of how theological reflection came to be a foundational part of theological education.

THE NEED FOR THEOLOGICAL REFLECTION

During their wilderness wandering, the children of Israel depended on God and Moses to provide for their needs. On one occasion, they were thirsty but there was no water for them to drink (Num. 20:2). No problem. God could meet this and any other need they would have. God told Moses exactly how to handle the situation: Moses was to grab his staff and, with his brother Aaron, assemble the people in front of the rock at Meribah. He was to speak to the rock, and God would provide water for the people and their livestock (Num. 20:8).

By now, Moses was a veteran ministry leader with a track record of success. Remember, he had just delivered the people from the grip of Pharaoh's tyranny. Not only was he building on past successes; he had everything he needed to be effective in this ministry challenge. Moses had a trusted ministry partner in Aaron. By his own admission, Moses was not a good public speaker (Ex. 6:30), but he had a ministry partner who could speak for the team. Like other effective ministry leaders, Moses was ministering out of his strengths and delegating for his weakness.

And then there was Moses's staff. Moses's staff may have looked like an ordinary walking stick, but it was far from ordinary. At the burning bush theophany, God told Moses to throw the staff to the ground. When Moses obeyed, the rod became a snake. Then God told him to pick up the snake by the tail. Again Moses obeyed, and the snake turned back into a staff (Ex. 4:2–4). With that staff, he initiated several of the plagues of Egypt (Ex. 7–11) and parted the Red Sea, allowing the children of Israel to escape from Egypt (Ex. 14).

With his ministry partner beside him and his trusted staff in his hand, Moses stood before the people ready to carry out a simple ministry assignment—speak to the rock, and God would provide water for the people.

WHAT'S WRONG?

"So Moses took the staff from the LORD's presence, just as he commanded him" (Num. 20:9). So far so good. "He and Aaron gathered the assembly together in front of the rock" (Num. 20:10a). Still good, right? But then it happened: "'Listen, you rebels, must we bring you water out of this rock?'

Then Moses raised his arm and struck the rock twice with his staff. Water gushed out, and the community and their livestock drank" (Num. 20:10b–11).

In the end, the people and the livestock drank. God came through for them, and they got the water they needed. In fact, the "water gushed out." It appeared to be an effective ministry. The need was met, and God's holiness was evident (Num. 20:13). What went wrong?

Effective Ministry Is Not Enough

Ministry effectiveness, as important as it is, is not enough.

In one sense, we could say, "mission accomplished." The thirsty people and livestock drank water that was gushing from a rock. But in another sense, this was one of Moses's lowest ministry moments. Because of his actions, he would be prohibited from leading the people into the promised land (Num. 20:12).

What went wrong? The people had a legitimate need that required intervention. They were thirsty and needed water. God had a plan. He told Moses to "speak to that rock before their eyes." Moses would speak, God would act, and the people would witness God providing for his people. Not only would their immediate needs be met, but they would be reminded that God was their provider who wasn't going to forsake them as they wandered through the wilderness. The older generation had forfeited their right to enter the promised land. But they were still God's people, and he would care for their needs.

Moses Speaks

It all went sideways when Moses began speaking. He said, "Listen, you rebels, must we bring you water out of this rock?" (Num. 20:10). Ouch, that's harsh. Not only did he deride them by calling them an unflattering name (rebels); he also belittled them for needing water and needing a leader. *Of course* they needed water—they were thirsty. *Of course* they needed a leader—they were wandering through life without purpose or an ultimate destination. They were walking in circles until they would die so the next generation could conquer the promised land that God had given them.

Moses left God out of his ministry execution. He did not even mention God. According to Moses, he and Aaron gave the people water.

Filled with anger, Moses ignored what God told him to do. Instead of speaking to the rock, he struck it. This was not the first time Moses's anger got him into trouble (Ex. 2).

Striking the rock instead of speaking was one thing, but the fact that Moses struck it with the staff that he took "from the LORD's presence" (Num. 20:9) was another. He struck the rock with the same staff that he used to initiate the plagues and command the Red Sea to part. The staff was not just a walking stick; it was an instrument that God worked through. With that holy staff, Moses struck the rock not once but twice.

What Was Happening inside and around Moses?

Moses's disobedience did not happen in a vacuum. He was going through a rough time.

He had just buried his sister Miriam (Num. 20:1) and was facing growing opposition from the people he served. "Now there was no water for the community, and the people gathered in opposition to Moses and Aaron" (Num. 20:2). You would have thought that right after Moses buried his sister, the people would have come together to support and encourage him, but they didn't. They did not assemble *for* their leaders. They assembled *against* them.

Moses was grieving, and the people were not helping matters with their constant complaining (Ps. 106:32–33). Yet Moses was still responsible to obey God and serve the people. God didn't give him a free pass by thinking, "Well, Moses is under a lot of pressure lately, so I'll just ignore his disobedience."

By striking the rock and claiming to be the one that was providing the water, Moses left God out of the picture. He made the moment all about himself. At Meribah, Moses broke faith with God (Deut. 32:51), contended with God (Deut. 33:8), and disobeyed God (Num. 27:14).

Moses's disobedience was not just a personal matter between him and God. It was not just about his spiritual health and relationship with God. He failed in his ministry practice. He did not apply the resources of faith to ministry.[5] It was not enough that his ministry was successful, that the

---

5. Theologians and ethicists alike underscore the importance of believers applying the tenets of their faith to their life choices. The doctrinal exposition of sanctification can be found in most evangelical systematic theologies, such as Millard Erickson, *Christian Theology*,

water gushed out of the rock. Neither was it enough that he knew what God wanted him to do. God requires obedience.

Our Ministry Actions Should Grow from Our Theology

What if Moses would have paused before he struck the rock? Would he have ministered differently? No doubt he was reacting out of his grief, frustration, and fatigue. We can only imagine what it felt like to hear the people pine for the good old days back in Egypt. In reality, they were saying that slavery under Pharaoh was better than freedom under Moses. It had to hurt. What if he had considered the faithfulness of God instead of the fickleness of the people? Holding the staff, he could have reflected on how God had used that very staff to free his people. Instead, in a fit of anger, he used it to belittle the people and rebel against God. What if Moses would have slowed down for just a minute? What if he would have paused?

The clear testimony of Scripture is that God requires obedience. Faithful ministry occurs when we close the gap between what we believe and how we actually live and minister. That discrepancy—the distance between our aspirational and actualized faith—is our growth potential. However, that gap is never closed without thoughtful reflection.

Closing the gap requires a pause in the action long enough to reflect and make adjustments before acting again. It is a pause to understand, yes,

---

3rd ed. (Grand Rapids: Baker, 2013); Wayne Grudem, *Systematic Theology* (Grand Rapids: Zondervan, 1994); Stanley Grenz, *Theology for the Community of God* (Grand Rapids: Eerdmans, 2000); and Michael Bird, *Evangelical Theology* (Grand Rapids: Zondervan, 2013). James Leo Garrett Jr., *Systematic Theology*, vol. 2, 2nd ed. (Eugene, OR: Wipf & Stock, 2014) is unique in supplying a chapter on Christian discipleship as a component of sanctification.

Christian ethics as a discipline deals extensively with the life God expects his children to live. Particularly helpful are volumes that seek to establish models for how to live the Christian life, versus ethics volumes that are more issues driven (i.e., how should a Christian respond to right to life issues?). The former include Dennis Hollinger, *Choosing the Good: Christian Ethics in a Complex World* (Grand Rapids: Baker Academic, 2002); Wyndy Corbin Reuschling, *Reviving Evangelical Ethics: The Promises and Pitfalls of Classic Models of Morality* (Grand Rapids: Brazos, 2008); Brian Brock, *Singing the Ethos of God: On the Place of Christian Ethics in Scripture* (Grand Rapids: Eerdmans, 2007); Richard Burridge, *Imitating Jesus: An Inclusive Approach to New Testament Ethics* (Grand Rapids: Eerdmans, 2007); David W. Gill, *Becoming Good: Building Moral Character* (Downers Grove, IL: InterVarsity Press, 2009); T. B. Maston, *Biblical Ethics: A Guide to the Ethical Message of the Scripture from Genesis through Revelation* (Macon, GA: Mercer University Press, 1997); Lewis Smedes, *Mere Morality: What God Expects from Ordinary People* (Grand Rapids: Eerdmans, 1989); and Joe Trull, *Walking in the Way: An Introduction to Christian Ethics* (Nashville: B&H, 1997).

But more than that, it is a pause to allow faith to shape ministry responses. Whether done individually or in community, a pause for theological reflection is necessary.

This book is about the pause.

That pause is more than just a vague space, bracketed by Christian ideals on one end and less-than-ideal responses on the other. Within the pause, a conversation must occur; it must continue among biblical and theological demands, personal and corporate experiences, and cultural realities of everyday life. The results of that conversation—undertaken with wisdom, honesty, courage, and integrity—will determine a ministry leader's response to leadership challenges.

The pages ahead show you what to do during the pause. You will learn how to create several types of ministry artifacts (journals, case studies, verbatim reports) and how to examine them in private moments, in one-on-one conversations, and with a group of peers. You will also encounter planning tools (covenant of learning, time and energy management) that will catalyze personal, spiritual, and professional growth.

But before we begin exploring the tools, let's pause for a moment to consider what theological reflection is.

CHAPTER 2

A DEFINITION OF THEOLOGICAL REFLECTION

At a Glance

- Theological reflection is modeled after a pattern found in the creation narrative.
- Theological reflection is a deeply spiritual activity requiring self-awareness, awareness of God's activities, a spirit of humility, and constant prayer.
- Theological reflection moves through three stages: identifying, aligning, and exploring.

THEOLOGICAL REFLECTION IS . . .

. . . *identifying* how our beliefs, thoughts, and feelings influence our actions, *aligning* them to our best understanding of God's truth, and *exploring* possibilities for future ministry responses.

This definition of theological reflection follows the "action—reflection—action" theological reflection approach. In this approach, reflection occurs during a pause from activity to learn from the past and prepare for the future. It follows the rhythm established in the opening pages of Scripture.

Genesis 1 contains multiple examples of God pausing to reflect on his creative activity. By the third day of creation, God concluded that his creation was good and that the earth should produce vegetation and fruit, which he gave a similar evaluation; it too "was good" (Gen. 1:10, 12). In like fashion, he created light on the fourth day and paused long enough to observe the goodness of his work (Gen. 1:18). Again, on the fifth day God created and then paused, observing what he had done, and then gave it the same positive evaluation: it was good (Gen. 1:21). On the sixth day, he created man, reflected upon his creation, and said this too was good—in fact, he said his creation was "very good" (Gen. 1:31).

The second chapter opens with God pausing to establish the Sabbath day as a holy, blessed day. Then the narrative flashes back and provides more information about the details of the sixth day. For the first time in the creation narrative, God commented that something was not good. "The LORD God said, 'It is not good for the man to be alone. I will make a helper suitable for him'" (Gen. 2:18). Out of this observation of a previous action came a resolve for a new action: the forming of a suitable helper for Adam.

The creation narrative includes times of reflection that separate future actions from those in the past. The process moved to a beat: action—reflection—action. The reflection separated the action. That is the rhythm of theological reflection.

Before exploring the definition further, it is important to underscore that theological reflection requires God's guidance. The entire process must be bathed in prayer and guided by the Holy Spirit. Theological reflection cannot be done effectively without God's help. Each of the following comments must be understood in light of this observation.

REFLECTION

In the simplest terms, reflection is pausing from activity long enough to think. Ministers should not pause to think about their actions in a previous ministry encounter for sentimental reasons. They should reflect on past activity so they can discover if it was as effective as it could have been and how they can minister in ways that are more aligned with their understanding of God's truth. This approach makes for a richer, deeper, more intentional, and honest reflective experience than merely reminiscing. Also, reflecting critically in order to be more effective in ministry completes the *reflection loop* (chap. 3). Theological reflection involves thinking backwards to assess past ministry actions and then applying that experience with honest critique to present and future ministry opportunities.

Good reflection also demands that ministers do something. The reflection process must result in a future action taken. The reflection process moves from observing and analyzing to doing.[1] It is intended to better prepare ministers for future ministry situations that demand action; that is why the minister undertakes the process. Action is the goal of reflection.

Good reflection is not limited to personal reflection. Outside voices enrich the process. Personal research and reading provide weight, contour, and necessary critique for the reflection process. Furthermore, doing the hard work of bringing in outside sources can take reflection deeper than the level of mere "spontaneous reflection."[2]

Spontaneous reflection implies that ministers engage theological reflection in an almost involuntary way, as a default process when ministry situations arise. No doubt, that is a good thing and is especially useful in journaling (chap. 5). However, in another sense, spontaneous reflection limits the reflection process to initial, random thoughts and self-suggestion, without consulting other helpful sources (biblical, theological, and theoretical). Reflection should move beyond the spontaneous.

Reflection Influences Future Actions

This "action—reflection—action" approach is in sharp contrast to "theology-in-action,"[3] which began in a Latin American context, nurtured

---

1. Pete Ward, *Introducing Practical Theology* (Grand Rapids: Baker Academic, 2017), 95.

2. Patricia O'Connell Killen and John de Beer, *The Art of Theological Reflection* (New York: Crossroad, 1994), 52. A simple example of spontaneous reflection could run along the following lines. A parishioner visits his pastor about the frustration he is feeling toward a coworker who continually belittles him at work. A spontaneous, ill-considered response from the pastor, reflecting very little true reflection, could be, "Well, the Bible says to love your neighbor, so just love your coworker and everything will be just fine." Rather, a disciplined, considered, thorough process of theological reflection could yield appropriate, creative, focused, effective ways to indeed love the coworker and thus minister to the distressed parishioner.

3. Elaine Graham, Heather Walton, and Frances Ward, *Theological Reflection: Methods* (London: SCM, 2005), 170. This term is used by Graham, Walton, and Ward to point to a unique understanding of practice and experience as sources of theological knowledge. Specifically, "theology-in-action" refers to placing fundamental and foundational value on such ministry practice: "Proper theological understanding cannot be formed independently of practical engagement."

by educators and theologians who worked to liberate the socially and eco-nomically oppressed.[4] Oppressed groups tended to think their oppressors withheld "true knowledge" and viewed orthodox theological propositions and traditional lecture-based education as the suspicious tools of capi-talist oppressors.[5] The only trustworthy information, from their point of view, is what inspires "restless, impatient, continuing, hopeful inquiry."[6] As Paulo Freire writes, *"Apart from the praxis*, individuals cannot be truly human."[7] To them, action/practice/praxis is the source of true education, true theological understanding, and true ministry practice. These groups taught that theoretical concepts, and even the theological propositions from systematic theology, are valuable only to the degree that they help guide critical reflection on practice. In summary, in the theology-in-action approach, orthopraxis (right practice) trumps ortho-doxy (right belief).

Our approach is different. We focus on altering future ministry actions, not current beliefs.

Reflection Changes the Minister

Theological reflection not only changes the way we approach ministry but also affects who we are as ministers. When done right, reflection transforms us, helping us become the kind of people God wants us to be. It emerges from the intersection of ministers' experiences and their inter-action with the Scriptures. This is especially important since "we minister out of who we are."[8]

---

4. Paulo Freire is the prime educational theorist. See Freire, *Pedagogy of the Oppressed*, trans. Myra Bergman Ramos, 30th anniv. ed. (New York: Continuum International, 2000). Liberation theology is the theological category created by this group. See Juan-Luis Segundo, *The Liberation of Theology* (New York NY: Orbis, 1976), among others. Historians of this approach to reflection locate its beginnings in early twentieth-century Roman Catholic Latin America in the Catholic Youth Workers movement, prior to Freire and liberation theology. See Ward, *Introducing Practical Theology*, 96; and Graham, Walton, and Ward, *Theological Reflection*, 183. Yet Freire and liberation theologians took the earlier work and crafted a robust and fully orbed framework for this approach to theological reflection.

5. Freire calls this the "banking" concept of education, whereby education consists only of teachers filling or "banking" their students with data: "The scope of the action allowed to the students extends only as far as receiving, filing, and storing the deposits." Freire, *Pedagogy of the Oppressed*, 72.

6. Freire, *Pedagogy of the Oppressed*, 72.

7. Freire, *Pedagogy of the Oppressed*, 72, emphasis added.

8. John Patton, "Some Reflections on Theological Reflection," *The Journal of Christian Ministry* 2 (2010): 2.

Paul Ballard says that believers are informed, guided, and fed by the Word; they know it, meditate on it, use it, and submit themselves to it. Ballard expands this idea, saying that theological reflection is more than just a technique to provide a quick ministry fix.[9] The disciple's life—the outflow of a vibrant relationship with God—is the ground of practice and preparation to do theological reflection well[10] and should produce spiritual growth.[11]

Robert Kinast uses the phrase "enacting the learning" to illustrate what reflection can do *for the minister.* He sees ministry action as having an impact on the minister's personal life, with the successful enacting of a ministry plan affecting who the minister is as a person (personal enacting), how future ministry activities are performed (ministerial enacting), and even how the minister thinks, knows, and perceives going forward (theological enactment).[12] Patricia O'Connell Killen and John de Beer agree, noting that the concluding action can bring about

> a deepening confirmation of a truth we have long accepted. It can be a different perspective that sheds light on a complex of feelings or behaviors with which we struggle. It can be a shift in attitude or emotion that frees us to live with a different tone or quality. It can be an intense insight that leaves us in a new world, a place far more textured and rich than we ever noticed before.[13]

---

9. "Theological reflection is simply an extension of the life of faith." Paul Ballard, "The Bible in Theological Reflection: Indication of the History of Scripture," *Practical Theology* 4, no. 1 (2011): 45, http://ezproxy.ccu.edu:2082/ehost /pdfviewer/ pdfviewer?vid=5&sid=2 c994843–1480–4bd0–8361–388400e7ba79%40sessionmgr4008. The context of Ballard's comment is a conversation about using Scripture as a critical source for theological reflection. Thus his assumption is that ministers have Scripture nearby. Ministers must possess a "level of biblical literacy that automatically informs thinking and praying, not simply as quotes but as an [sic] *habitus*, an instinctive wisdom."

10. Paul Ballard, "Theological Reflection and Providence," *Practical Theology* 1, no. 3 (2009): 288.

11. Robert Mulholland and Ruth Haley Barton define spiritual disciplines as "the practices the church has come to realize are essential for deepening one's relationship with God, enriching one's life with others and nurturing one toward wholeness in Christ." Mulholland and Barton, *Invitation to a Journey: A Roadmap for Spiritual Formation*, exp. ed. (Downers Grove, IL: InterVarsity Press, 2016), 90. Faithfully practiced, theological reflection can accomplish all those goals for the minister.

12. Robert Kinast, *Let Ministry Teach: A Guide to Theological Reflection* (Collegeville, MN: Liturgical, 1996), 152–64.

13. Killen and de Beer, *Art of Theological Reflection*, 67.

This range of effects on the minister, who undertakes theological reflection to its preferred end, again points to spiritual formation in the minister's own life—being conformed to the image of Jesus (Rom. 8:29) and moving down the road of a "journey into intensification" in the life of faith.[14]

IDENTIFYING HOW OUR BELIEFS, THOUGHTS, AND FEELINGS INFLUENCE OUR ACTIONS

Theological reflection begins "in the middle of things."[15] The minister approaches a ministry opportunity situated firmly in the middle of multiple realities, in the middle of a specific congregation, a larger community, family relationships, ministry relationships, (chronologically) an increasingly complex problem or situation that began and developed before the minister arrived, and (theologically) a situation that lands in the middle of multiple doctrines. Ministers must take into account all these "middles" as they begin responding well.

Beyond the external reality of being "in the middle of things," ministers are also in the middle of things in their own lives. They are in the middle of God forming them spiritually, participating in their families, churches, and communities, and other ministry encounters. All of these dynamics can affect the ministers' assessment of the situation at hand. Self-assessment helps ministers know to what degree they can put themselves into the reflection process and their ministry action plan.[16]

Beliefs Influence Actions

Ministers' self-assessment of their personal beliefs is critical. What they believe across the entire spectrum of theological understanding—from

---

14. Killen and de Beer, *Art of Theological Reflection*, 67.

15. Rowan Williams, *On Christian Theology* (Oxford: Blackwell, 2000), xii, quoted in Ward, *Introducing Practical Theology*, 10. Ward presents this idea in the context of a "doing theology" approach to theological reflection, but the idea fits our approach also. For more information on "doing theology" see Trevor Hart, *Faith Thinking: The Dynamics of Christian Theology* (Eugene, OR: Wipf & Stock, 1995), 189: "Doing theology" refers to the usage of theological ideas as ongoing, formative concepts which direct the Christian church (from individual Christians to local churches to denominational bodies) to be faithfully what it was created to be. Hart describes the central task of doing theology as "translation of the gospel into forms which are meaningful for our spatial and temporal context, that those who live alongside us in that context may hear and understand and discover the relevance and meaning of the gospel for themselves."

16. Ward, *Introducing Practical Theology*, 116.

the doctrine of God to eschatology—determines their ministry practice.[17] Belief systems should determine how ministers live and minister.[18] So, for example, what ministers believe about the Christian institution of marriage will determine how they assess and reflect theologically upon the ministry opportunity of counseling same-sex couples. Their understanding of grace should influence how they treat church staff members who make mistakes, among other things.

Thoughts Influence Actions

A minister begins the thinking process by asking this question: What is really going on in this ministry situation?[19] Killen and de Beer call this the "heart of the matter"—that is, defining "the central question, tension, issue, theme, problem or [even] wonderment of an experience."[20] This critical and foundational assessment of the situation requires honest, thorough, and focused thought.

Thinking involves more than assessing the situation; it also is an attempt to use reason, logic, and understanding to benefit the minister and those being ministered to. "The usefulness of reason as a theological resource has to do with taking care in how we think about things."[21] Debates have raged throughout Christian history about the proper relationship between reason and theology, begun perhaps by the apostle Paul ("knowledge puffeth up," 1 Cor. 8:1 KJV; cf. Paul's use of philosophy in Acts 17), carried on by Tertullian ("What has Athens to do with Jerusalem?"), and perpetuated by many Christian leaders through the years. Where ministers get their data, how they employ it, and how their

---

17. Howard W. Stone and James O. Duke, *How to Think Theologically* (Minneapolis: Fortress, 2006), 45ff. While we emphasize three things (believe, think, and feel), Stone and Duke suggest resources consistent with the Wesleyan Quadrilateral: Scripture, tradition, reason, and experiences.

18. Miroslav Volf, *Captive to the Word of God: Engaging the Scriptures for Contemporary Theological Reflection* (Grand Rapids: Eerdmans., 2010), 50: "Christian beliefs are not simply statements about what was, is, and will be the case; they are statements about what *should* be the case and what human beings should do about that. They provide a normative vision for practices."

19. This question, "What is going on?" is actually the first step in a theological reflection process attributed to Richard Osmer, as noted in Ward, *Introducing Practical Theology*, 98.

20. Killen and de Beer, *Art of Theological Reflection*, 61. The authors utilize this term in the context of pursuing one's own experience as the almost exclusive arena of doing theological reflection. Nevertheless, the term works here too.

21. Stone and Duke, *How to Think Theologically*, 52.

theological commitments guide its use are germane. But based on the assumptions that (1) Christians' minds as well as their souls are redeemed and (2) all truth is grounded in God, reason can then be seen as a legitimate conversation partner in theological reflection. What ministers *think* is an important part of the reflection process. Ministers should strive to make their theological reflection as "clear, coherent, and well informed as possible."[22]

Feelings Influence Actions

Killen and de Beer advocate that the first step in theological reflection is to enter into one's own experiences, "describing from inside the evidence of our own senses."[23] "This is theological reflection—to allow the thoughts, feelings, images, and insights that arise from the concrete events of our lives to be in genuine conversation with the wisdom of the Christian community throughout the ages."[24] Though the intense inward focus of this starting point seems subjective, it is valuable for ministers to take a deep dive into their personal contexts, commitments, relationships, and roles as an assessment exercise to help set a good course for theological reflection.

We are not promoting a contemplative spirituality that encourages reflection in the pursuit of a mystical experience with God. While theological reflection does include paying attention to the inner world, it does not elevate subjective observations to the level of authoritative insights. All reflective activities are balanced by the objective standard of God's truth as revealed in God's Word.

This kind of balance between subjective and objective can be observed in Paul's instruction to the Philippians. While they were to reflect on the best of their culture, they were also to put into practice what they had received and learned from Paul and had seen exhibited in his life.[25] Reflection and life-application must be filtered through the authoritative witness found in the Scriptures. This is best done in the

---

22. Stone and Duke, *How to Think Theologically*, 53.
23. Killen and de Beer, *Art of Theological Reflection*, 17.
24. Killen and de Beer, *Art of Theological Reflection*, 18.
25. Gordon D. Fee, *Philippians*, IVP New Testament Commentary 11 (Downers Grove, IL: InterVarsity Press, 1999), 178.

context of fellow believers, always remembering that we are to "comprehend with all the saints what is the breadth and length and height and depth" (Eph. 3:18 ESV). Truth and our understanding of it are in the realm of "all the saints," not just the individual believer. The believing community provides the safeguard that keeps our reflections balanced and on track.

However, if we do not look inside, we can miss an important source of information that benefits the reflection process. For instance, sometimes we *react* when we should *respond* to a ministry situation. Have you ever become irritated and snapped at someone without knowing why? Most of us have been less than gracious because we were tired and frustrated. That reaction does not emanate from what we believe; most ministers agree that we should be kind to everyone (Eph. 4:32). Neither does it come from what we think; education theory does not suggest that people learn better when their ministers are short with them. While understanding that being overly tired and experiencing frustration does not excuse boorish behavior, it does inform how we should respond the next time we find ourselves fatigued in a ministry context. In reflection, once we identify what we were feeling, we can come up with a response more in line with our theology and understanding of educational theory.

This process requires prayer, wisdom, insight, knowledge, focus, clarity, and patience. The kind of patience needed at this stage resists defaulting into past ministry.[26] Clarity, again, is needed to see this current situation as unique and in varying degrees separate from anything similar—past or future. Past experiences and future projections will play roles in the problem assessment, but they also must be distinguished from the unique present.

Given all "the middles" in which ministers are situated, it is critical to narrow, focus, define, and clarify the issue—or to use our key word, *identify* the "heart of the matter"—not only for aiming at a preferred ministry solution but also for properly beginning the process of theological reflection.

---

26. Paul Ballard, "Reflections on Theological Reflection," *Modern Believing* 40, no. 3 (July 1999): 16.

ALIGNING THEM TO OUR BEST UNDERSTANDING OF GOD'S TRUTH

Scripture Is God's Truth

Scripture should be the first and primary source for the reflection process. Furthermore, to speak of "God's truth" is to refer primarily to the biblical record. Since this is the case, it is important to clarify our convictions about Scripture.

The Bible is the self-revelation of God. In it, he reveals who he is (Ex. 3:13–14; 34:6–7; John 1:14), what he's done in history (Ps. 78:4; Col. 1:22), and what he will do in the future (Rev. 1:4). These statements contrast with the view that the Bible is primarily a "handbook for Christian living," or even an answer book for theological reflection. To reduce Scripture to an encyclopedia about my problems is to cloud God's revelation to us. God is essentially hidden, mysterious, and holy, yet he intends to be known by human beings. God must initiate the disclosure and has done so by acting in ways to make himself known.[27] The Bible is about God primarily, and it is about people to the degree that they are involved in God's story.

Resetting the perspective on what the Bible actually is—God's story—does not require abandoning it as a guide for living, however. Miroslav Volf says that people should approach Scripture with a "hermeneutic of respect"—that is, an "attitude of receptivity" and belief, commensurate with the fact that God has revealed himself in its pages.[28] He continues:

> We read it expecting that by finding ourselves and our world in the story of God's dealings with humanity, we will (re)discover our true identities and the world's proper destiny. We study it anticipating that we will discover the wisdom to help individuals, communities, and our entire planet genuinely to flourish. We read it trusting that we will learn better to love God and neighbor.[29]

Therefore, the Bible helps us reflect theologically on God, who he is, what he tells us about human behavior (Ps. 119:9), how he has redeemed

---

27. Fisher Humphreys, *Thinking about God*, 2nd ed. (New Orleans, LA: Insight Press, 1994), 14–16.
28. Volf, *Captive to the Word of God*, 34.
29. Volf, *Captive to the Word of God*, 34.

humans through the work of Jesus Christ (Luke 1:68), and what he might be doing in the ministry situation at hand (Rev. 21:5). The Bible reveals God's presence among us, living and active in words people can understand.

Scripture also exposes how people "tried and failed to live out their calling."[30] Abraham and Moses are often worth imitating; Jephthah and Samson, not so much. Jesus and Paul provide guidance; Judas Iscariot and Ananias, well . . . no. Especially for ministers' reflective processes, the Bible reflects our story, showing us the way through good and bad examples of human response to God.

As the key resource for theological reflection, Scripture exposes who we are. The Bible is primarily the self-revealing, personal disclosure of God, but secondarily it is a guide to understanding human behavior, exposing "the thoughts and attitudes of the heart" (Heb. 4:12). The Bible presents a different approach to living life and doing ministry (Isa. 55:8). Walter Brueggemann says, "The Bible provides us with an alternative identity, an alternative way of understanding ourselves, an alternative way of relating to the world. It offers a radical and uncompromising challenge to our ordinary ways of self-understanding."[31] For the minister, this means being willing to challenge every idea—preconceived, traditional, comfortable, denominational, cultural, communal, and reasonable—if God so directs through his Word, rightly understood and interpreted. The Bible is *that* important to theological reflection.

The primary source of truth, especially for the reflection process, is Holy Scripture. The Bible contains God's ultimate self-revelation in the life, ministry, death, and resurrection of Jesus, God the Son, the living Word of God, the Redeemer of all creation. To the degree that God interacts with humans and humans respond to him, the Bible also acts as a guide for such response. Scripture shows both good and bad responses to divine leadership, but what is most important for ministers seeking the truth about God is whether they will willingly, believingly, and courageously follow that truth in their ministry responses.

---

30. Ballard, "The Bible in Theological Reflection," 38.
31. Walter Brueggemann, *The Bible Makes Sense* (Louisville: Westminster John Knox, 2001), 10; cited in Ballard, "The Bible in Theological Reflection," 43.

All Truth Is God's Truth

Claims about the primacy of Scripture in theological reflection do not exclude using truth found outside the Bible as a resource for theological reflection. There are insights and realities about life and relationships that can be gained from the social sciences, literature, the arts, and philosophy that can assist the believer in understanding the things of God and how he is active in the world at all times (John 5:17, 19–20). This concept is grounded in the reality that God is omnipotent, omniscient, and omnipresent, so we can view all of life as theological. As we live and minister, we should seek to be aware of how our faith affects our interaction with the world, how we respond in specific situations, and where and how we experience God.

Augustine affirmed that all truth is God's truth.[32] The truth of a situation, the truth applicable from various sources scientific or literary, and the truth about oneself all come to bear on the ministry situation.

Stanley Grenz positions his understanding of the manifold sources of truth in the universal work of God the Holy Spirit, confessing his ubiquitous presence and activity. "Consequently [the Spirit] can speak through many media." Yet true to his high view of Scripture, Grenz adds quickly that the Spirit speaks "only and always in accordance with, and never contrary to, Biblical truth." The context of Grenz's comments is his affirmation that God can speak truth through pop culture media, but his larger point is to encourage the "use of contemporary 'knowledge' in the theological task." Grenz writes, "Our theological reflection can draw from the so-called 'secular' sciences, because ultimately no truth is, in fact, secular."[33]

EXPLORING POSSIBILITIES FOR FUTURE MINISTRY RESPONSES

Future ministry opportunities are not necessarily hazy points on a far-off horizon. Sometimes they come within hours of the most recent ministry encounter. Because ministers never know when the next ministry

---

32. Augustine's actual quote is, "Let every good and true Christian understand that wherever truth may be found, it belongs to his Master." Augustine, *On Christian Doctrine* 2.18.28, in *A Select Library of the Nicene and Post-Nicene Fathers of the Christian Church*, vol. 2, *St. Augustin's City of God and Christian Doctrine* (Buffalo, NY: Christian Literature Company, 1887), 545.

33. Stanley Grenz, *Theology for the Community of God* (Grand Rapids: Eerdmans, 2000), 310.

situation, opportunity, or difficulty will appear, they must begin the reflection process while the ministry encounter is fresh and continue it into the future. Theological reflection is not so much a box to check on a ministerial to-do list as it is a near and constant process that ministers use to *align* their actions with their best understanding of God's truth.

Another guide in this phase of *exploring possibilities for future ministry responses* is simply patience—waiting until the proper solution or appropriate guidance arrives. This type of waiting is not the same as trying to wait patiently until the mechanic completes the brake job on your car. Stone and Duke correlate waiting with listening. Allowing new and varied sources into the conversation is the "active waiting" required to listen well.[34] Listening not only to Scripture and tradition but also to God the Holy Spirit often requires patience and a desire to hear, so humility is required even here. These qualities are included in "active waiting."

While we do not view action as a primary source of theological knowledge ("theology-in-action" approach), we do affirm that doing something is the final and necessary step for an effective theological reflection process.

The types of action that conclude a theological reflection process are as varied as the ministry that precipitates the process. As a result of reflecting theologically on a situation, a minister may pray with sharper focus, counsel with greater clarity, confront with deeper courage, proclaim with stronger conviction . . . the list goes on.

However, the action to which a theological reflection process leads is much more than the final step in a process and much more than a solution to a ministerial conundrum. The minister's hope is that the people involved in a ministry situation are benefited directly, growing in their faith by experiencing the ministering presence of God through the minister's reflective and responsive ministry action.

This reflective and responsive ministry action benefits its direct recipients, but it also builds up others. By a ripple effect, the greater faith community and even the larger community in which the church resides can benefit, responding perhaps as the people of the Decapolis responded to a former demon-possessed man. "And he went away and

---

34. Stone and Duke, *How to Think Theologically*, viii.

began to proclaim . . . how much Jesus had done for him, *and everyone marveled*" (Mark 5:20 ESV, emphasis added). Ministry action, through an effective process of theological reflection, can have powerful and far-reaching effects.[35]

Finally, ministers must be open to new possibilities and even "strange connections" as they pursue God's direction in dealing with a particular ministry issue.[36] If they already knew what needed to happen, then theological reflection would not be necessary. So even though they will pursue reasonable and obvious directions toward determining a solution, ministers must be open to God redirecting them in ways only God could know.

In a sense, ministers take a risk when they reflect on God's Word, seek wisdom through prayer, and consult other trusted sources. The outcome of such reflection may be radically different than what they expected at the outset of the process, but the risk must be taken for theological reflection to bear mature fruit. Such "risky behavior" is synonymous with what Tod Bolsinger calls "adaptive capacity"—the ability to respond effectively to new situations amid changing dynamics, or the capacity to adapt and minister well.[37]

---

35. Graham, Walton, and Ward posit their goals for doing theology (the macro view of theological reflection) by means of this same set of concentric circles: individuals growing in discipleship, the church being built and sustained, and the "wider culture" hearing the faith. Graham, Walton, and Ward, *Theological Reflection*, 10ff.

36. Ballard, "Reflections on Theological Reflection," 14.

37. Tod Bolsinger, *Canoeing the Mountains: Christian Leadership in Uncharted Territory* (Downers Grove, IL: InterVarsity Press, 2015), 90. Among the "set of skills to be mastered" in exercising adaptive capacity are refusing "quick fixes," seeking "new perspectives," and asking questions "that reveal competing values and gaps in values and actions." These are helpful skills for theological reflection too. Apparently, Bolsinger borrowed the term "adaptive capacity" from Ronald A. Heifitz, Marty Linsky, and Alexander Grashow, *The Practice of Adaptive Leadership: Tools and Tactics for Changing Your Organization and the World* (Boston: Harvard Business School Press, 2009).

CHAPTER 3

A MODEL FOR THEOLOGICAL REFLECTION

At a Glance

- Our theological reflection model, the reflection loop, draws on the strengths of other reflection models.
- To better understand the reflection loop, a brief survey of other models that influenced the development of ours is provided.
- The reflection loop guides ministers as they pause from ministry activity to do meaningful theological reflection.

Theological reflection models are valuable because they contribute to an ongoing discussion among practical theologians about how to apply theology to their lives and ministry. Even when a specific model fails to explain everything involved in the reflection activity, it furthers the conversation. Before introducing the reflection loop, our theological reflection model, we want to put it into a context with other significant models. Each of these models contributed to our understanding of the theological reflection process and the development of our model.

OTHER THEOLOGICAL REFLECTION MODELS

Whitehead Model

Attending—Asserting—Decision

The appropriate starting place is the Whitehead model. James and Evelyn Whitehead developed one of the first theological reflection models of the modern era.[1] In their model, the Whiteheads brought together three resources to aid ministers in reflection: the ministers' *experiences*, their *culture*, and *Christian tradition*. In reflection, ministers listen, or "attend," to all three, noting both positive and negative contributions. Such "attending" moves to "asserting" (bringing all three into conversation) and results in "decision," or action.[2] The theological reflection models that follow, including ours, echo the movements their model established.

McCarty Model
Analyze—Consider—Decide

Doran McCarty defined theological reflection as "a person's interaction with experience taking into account various aspects of reality and faith and the presence of God."[3] McCarty illustrated his original model with a "history-head-heart" triangle. The second iteration of the model expanded the diagram to a "history-head-heart-holy" diamond. The addition of the "holy" accounted for the work of the Holy Spirit and considerations from Scripture.

Within that diamond, ministers were to analyze data from sociology, psychology, their physical senses, economics, politics, traditions, psychology, theology, culture, memories, dreams, and relationships. After analyzing a ministry event in light of these disciplines, McCarty taught that ministers could consider their ministry activities in light of who they are—their backgrounds, values, personality types, the work of the Holy Spirit, and their potential effectiveness. After analyzing and considering these things, ministers can then decide a course of action. McCarty's model emphasized that the time of reflection should end in a more

---

1. Edward Foley, "Reflective Believing: Reimagining Theological Reflection in an Age of Diversity," *Reflective Practice: Formation and Supervision in Ministry* 34 (2014): 61: "It is widely acknowledged that James and Evelyn Whitehead were pioneers here."

2. James D. Whitehead and Evelyn Eaton Whitehead, *Method in Ministry: Theological Reflection and Christian Ministry* (New York: Seabury, 1980).

3. Doran C. McCarty, "Theological Reflection," *Supervised Ministry* (Mill Valley, CA: Golden Gate Baptist Theological Seminary, 1982), 7.

informed, intentional ministry that emanates from who the minister is.[4] He says, "The effectiveness of a minister is in his/her ability to minister intentionally on the basis of his/her theological reflection."[5]

Narrative Theology–Based Model

Speak—Write—Act

Graham, Walton, and Ward's *Theological Reflection: Methods* presents a set of frameworks or approaches for doing theology that focused on narrative theology. They identified this source of reflection as "speaking in parables." They observed that Jesus's parables not only disarmed their hearers but also communicated to them in deeply personal and effective ways. Stories across the spectrum of media—from literature (e.g., Bunyan's *Pilgrim's Progress*) to films (e.g., *Diary of a City Priest*)—can be powerful conveyors of truth too. There are certain truths wrapped up in "the mysterious and indefinable aspects of human experience" that can be communicated best through story.[6]

The power of story also applies to ministers' own stories and their stories' benefit for theological reflection. Stories can become a living record, useful for understanding life and ministry. What can those stories contribute to a better understanding of the personalities interacting in a ministry situation? Can the people involved better convey their understanding of the situation through story? Can a narrative approach to a ministry situation not only convey truth but also enable all participants to drop their defenses and move closer to a resolution as their stories are articulated, received, and valued?

Stories are helpful at the corporate level too. Graham, Walton, and Ward called this "Writing the Body of Christ," thus proposing a form of corporate theological reflection. Their context suggested the practice of a local congregation coming together to create a corporate identity around a central motif or metaphor, based on their shared story. Their examples

---

4. The McCarty Model was my (Wilson) first exposure to theological reflection and has been the basis of what we have taught in Gateway's DMin program prior to the development of the reflection loop. Traces of his model remain in ours.

5. McCarty, "Theological Reflection," 7–10.

6. Elaine Graham, Heather Walton, and Frances Ward, *Theological Reflection: Methods* (London: SCM, 2005), 47.

ranged from base communities in Latin America to the emergent church. An example from local church ministry could be a church that identifies intentionally with its community or prime ministry objective, like the Church of the Open Door (Los Angeles, CA) or the Church That Never Closes (Reformed Church of Prince Bay, Staten Island, NY).[7]

The idea of corporate theological reflection can point in a different direction, not just to the constructing of a unique local church identity but also to the engaging of a minister with the church's identity. Every church has a story, and knowing that story well can provide abundant resources for the reflective minister. "*Paying attention* to the sights, smells, and tastes of communal life will lead the pastor into a much richer and more complex understanding of the cultural narratives of the community."[8]

Ministers can also engage the church's story through ethnographic studies by listening intentionally and systematically to the unique cultural realities of a congregation as "a means to immerse oneself in the life of people to learn something about them and from them."[9] For example, knowing the complex story of a congregation can assist the minister in reflecting effectively on why newly married couples who have deep roots in their church's life are either struggling or flourishing in their relationships. The corporate story can also point the pastor to the seeds of a long-simmering congregational rift or to the real story behind the people's reticence to enter into a building program, sing or not sing certain songs, or adopt a new discipleship approach.

Pastoral Cycle Model

See—Judge—Act

The pastoral cycle[10] is essentially a three-phased approach to doing theology: *see, judge,* and *act.* The ministers *see* the situation, *judge* what needs to be done, and *act* accordingly.[11] The cycle continues as the need

---

7. Graham, Walton, and Ward, *Theological Reflection,* 109–37.

8. Pete Ward, *Introducing Practical Theology* (Grand Rapids: Baker Academic, 2017), 112, emphasis added.

9. Ward, *Introducing Practical Theology,* 112.

10. Graham, Walton, and Ward, *Theological Reflection,* 188–91; Ward, *Introducing Practical Theology,* 96ff.

11. *See* can refer to the observation of the ministry *act* of the previous round of the cycle.

for theological reflection continues. Literature on theological reflection often champions the pastoral cycle as the preferred and paradigmatic way to do theological reflection. Yet one assumption at the heart of the cycle conflicts with the values of most evangelical ministers. "The pastoral cycle assumes that each new reality or problem is calling people of faith to reinterpret the Word of God anew, but that theology, in the form of received tradition (doctrine, Bible, church traditions) needs to be reinterpreted in the light of contemporary faith and tested against insights from other cultures and disciplines."[12]

This reinterpretation of received tradition is troublesome to evangelical thinkers insomuch as the situation and the minister determine what theology *is* even to the extent of refashioning "doctrine, Bible, [and] Church traditions." Refashioning Scripture is not an option for us and likely not an option for most of our evangelical readers. Furthermore, given the hyperconstructive nature in its original form of *see, judge, act*, this approach may not even require traditional theological ideas from orthodox theological resources. There is nothing inherently theological about those three verbs, so again the cycle is only theological to the degree that the minister wants it to be. As Ward notes, "So [with the pastoral cycle] theological reflection is placed outside the normal ways in which, by being part of the church, we are involved in the continual processes of theological reflection."[13]

With this caution, we acknowledge this model's value. If evangelical ministers bring their theological convictions to the pastoral cycle while understanding its contextual assumptions, the cycle can be a helpful reflection tool for doing theology.

One way the cycle influences other theological reflection models, including ours, is that it forces ministers to focus on action—action at the beginning of the process and action at the end. Theological reflection is the minister's response to a specific situation. And every ministry situation, of course, begins with some action having occurred. What is

---

Each subsequent version of a ministry act should be more appropriate and effective than the previous versions due to the appropriate *judgment*.

12. Graham, Walton, and Ward, *Theological Reflection*, 188.

13. Ward, *Introducing Practical Theology*, 100. Ward provided other criticisms of the pastoral cycle, but they point beyond the scope of this chapter (pp. 100–102).

that action? How best can the minister see and diagnose it? The pastoral cycle helps ministers identify the action that began this process in the first place. At the other end of the process, action must be the final step for any effective theological reflection process. Ultimately, fresh assessment and reassessment of ministry actions through repeated rounds of the cycle will result in better future ministry responses.

Four Tasks Model

Richard Osmer presented a four-step version of the pastoral cycle.[14] His questions provided good handles for process steps and pointed to larger task categories.[15] Here are both the questions and their respective categories:[16]

> **What is going on?** This is the "descriptive-empirical task," wherein diagnostic information on the situation is gathered.
> **Why is this going on?** The next step is the "interpretive task." This step utilizes "theories of the arts and sciences" to unpack the certain situation or situations identified in the previous step.[17]
> **What ought to be going on?** The third step is the "normative task." Here theological concepts are used as interpretive tools.
> **How might we respond?** The fourth and final step is the "pragmatic task." This is the step where action is undertaken.

Osmer's questions, as well as the pastoral cycle in general, can be helpful for ministers. Such a clear-cut, enumerated framework provides a clear process for undertaking theological reflection. It is also an effective framework for teaching reflection because of its clarity and simplicity. Once again, we emphasize the need for evangelicals to define

---

14. Richard R. Osmer, *Practical Theology: An Introduction* (Grand Rapids: Eerdmans, 2008). Pete Ward maintained that the pastoral cycle is the antecedent for Osmer's work, but Osmer never made this claim. See Ward, *Introducing Practical Theology*, 98.

15. Osmer asserted that his method "may be brought to bear on *any* issue worthy of consideration." See Osmer, *Practical Theology*, x. Therefore, Osmer's method may be considered an approach to doing theology or addressing specific ministry situations, the latter being the focus of our book.

16. Osmer, *Practical Theology*, 4. The outline is taken from page 4, but each question and its respective category comprise one of the book's four chapters.

17. Osmer, *Practical Theology*, 4.

the contours of the cycle according to their theological commitments, making sure that the cycle functions in theologically sound ways, particularly in making appropriate use of Scripture as the prime source of God's truth.

OUR MODEL: THE REFLECTION LOOP

Identify—Align—Explore

The reflection loop is a model built upon our definition of theological reflection explained in the previous chapter. According to the model, theological reflection is ***identifying*** *how our beliefs, thoughts, and feelings influence our actions,* ***aligning*** *them to our best understanding of God's truth, and* ***exploring*** *possibilities for future ministry responses.* As with the pastoral cycle, action surrounds the reflection loop. A ministry action leads into the loop and a new, better-informed action emerges from the loop.

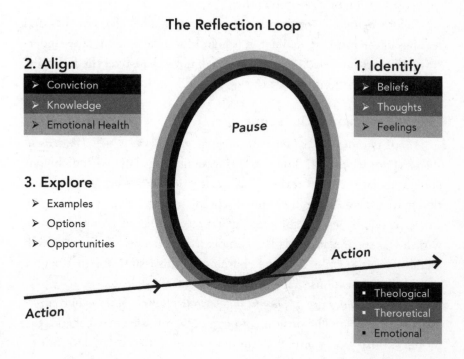

The Reflection Loop

2. Align
- ➢ Conviction
- ➢ Knowledge
- ➢ Emotional Health

1. Identify
- ➢ Beliefs
- ➢ Thoughts
- ➢ Feelings

Pause

3. Explore
- ➢ Examples
- ➢ Options
- ➢ Opportunities

Action

Action

- ▪ Theological
- ▪ Theroretical
- ▪ Emotional

Our definition of theological reflection states that our beliefs, thoughts, and feelings influence our actions and that we need to identify how they are influencing the actions. This is a positive statement about what should happen. However, there can be a discrepancy between our ideals and our behavior—when we fail to live up to what we believe, think, and feel.

In reality, we have two theologies: a confessional and an operational theology. The former we ascribe to, speak about, preach about, and believe in. The latter is the one we live. At the heart of theological reflection is a desire to close the gap between what we say we believe and how we live. This is true in our walk with God and in our ministry approaches. Therefore, while we do identify where our beliefs, thoughts, and feelings had a positive influence on our actions, we spend a majority of our time reflecting on where we failed to put them into practice. We ask not only which theology drove our actions but also which one *should have been* driving our actions.

Some reflection happens in real time during the ministry event, but the reflection loop is most useful when examining a past action as documented in a ministry artifact such as a journal entry (chap. 5), verbatim report (chap. 7), or case study (chap. 7).

Before *identifying* the details of the operational beliefs, thoughts, and feelings in the ministry artifact, it is helpful to take a moment to understand the surrounding key issues. Though not exhaustive, the following preliminary questions will lay the groundwork for identifying key issues.

Helpful Preliminary Questions

What is going on? What is the significance of the event? What is at stake? What is the cost? This set of questions looks beyond the obvious and immediate context of the ministry situation. For example, the situation may involve a church member's complaint regarding changes in the worship style. Does the complainant represent a larger group of people within the congregation? Is the complainant a deeply involved church member? Will people leave the church over this issue? To what degree should these questions shape the ministry solution?

What dynamics are at play in the various players? Who is in control? Who is vulnerable? The position of power in a ministry event shapes the proper ministry response. The minister, in an effort to achieve mutually beneficial solutions for multiple parties, may respond differently depending on who has inflicted wounds and who has been wounded. The power positions may reverse in the ministry situation. For example, if a wife abuses her husband, she is in control in the abuse scenario; she committed the abuse. However, in approaching a ministry solution, the abused husband assumes control; his perception and recounting of the event determine in large part how to arrive at a suitable resolution. Ministers must pay careful attention to who is in control and who is vulnerable throughout the entire course of the ministry situation.

What are the individual parts (the trees) of the experience (the forest)? This question focuses the minister's attention on the individual components of the ministry crisis, taking into account the potential effects of a solution on each stakeholder. How will the ministry solution affect each person involved?

How do the parts (the trees) affect the big picture (the forest)? Whereas the questions above represent analysis, synthesis considers broader issues rather than individual components. How will the ministry solution affect them rather than him or her? Ministers must consider both analysis and synthesis in seeking a successful ministry solution.

Does anyone else have a vantage point that needs consideration? Many ministry situations involve third-party stakeholders. These are less obvious players in a ministry situation—the people who may be wounded as collateral damage in a ministry crisis or experience a blessing as a ministry byproduct. How should the minister factor these people into the ministry solution? For example, in the Good Samaritan parable, the innkeeper would be a third-party stakeholder. The Samaritan understood that proper, ongoing care for the wounded traveler involved paying the innkeeper.

After identifying what happened in the ministry event by asking preliminary questions, ministers may turn their attention to identifying their operational beliefs, thoughts, and feelings.

IDENTIFYING HOW OUR BELIEFS, THOUGHTS, AND FEELINGS INFLUENCE OUR ACTIONS

Theological

The first step in the reflection loop requires *identifying* the gaps between our operational beliefs (as exemplified in our ministry actions) and our confessed beliefs. This step requires courage, lowering defenses, and a deep search for truth. It requires asking hard questions but is not an exercise in self-flagellation. The goal is not to feel bad about past behavior but to improve future actions.

In the parable of the Good Samaritan, Jesus helped his hearers understand the meaning of the word *neighbor* by telling a story about how three different people responded to a person in need. The priest and the Levite crossed the road to avoid the wounded man (Luke 10:31–32), but the Samaritan took care of the man's pressing needs, proving himself to be the neighbor (Luke 10:33–35). Even though the first two men in the story, the priest and the Levite, would have been well-equipped to explain the Jewish customs about how to treat sojourners (Ex. 2:20; Judg. 19:22; 1 Sam. 25:2–38; Isa. 58:7), they failed to live up to the ideals they espoused. Instead, the despised Samaritan lived out biblical values.

Theoretical

Theological reflection involves *identifying* the theological gap between our operational and confessional faith in our past ministries, but because all truth is God's truth, it also requires thinking on a theoretical level. We reflect on our theology in an attempt to minister in a right way, to minister righteously. We reflect on the theoretical gap between our operational and confessed theory in an attempt to have an effective, efficient, productive ministry.

In the parable, the Samaritan poured oil and wine on the victim's wounds before taking him to an inn (Luke 10:34), not for theological reasons but to cleanse the wound. He did immediate first aid using the items he had at his disposal. After meeting the injured man's immediate needs, the Samaritan put the man on his donkey and took him to get additional help.

Certainly the choice to help the man had deep theological roots. Beyond the concepts of caring for strangers and sojourners, issues of love, compassion, putting others first, and being a neighbor emerge. The Samaritan's actions (pouring wine and oil and binding the wounds) were undergirded by a theoretical base. The wine and oil cleansed the wounds and fought infection. Binding the wound stopped bleeding and protected it from outside contaminants.

Emotional

There is a third level worthy of examination: the emotional level. For most, seeing another person in need evokes an emotional response. Sometimes it triggers a flashback to an experience or a family of origin issue. Because emotions are strong drivers of ministry behavior and can hijack the best intentions or prompt risky actions, it is wise to examine what was going on in our interior world during a ministry incident. As far as the parable goes, many of us have heard sermons that speculate as to why the priest and the Levite passed by on the other side. Most of those speculations examine their emotional reactions or their current state of mind. While speculation on another person's emotions has some utility, the real benefit of identifying the operational emotional state is to enable *self*-examination.

SOME HELPFUL QUESTIONS

In the section below we suggest some helpful *identifying*, *aligning* and *exploring* questions. This is not an exhaustive list or a list of questions that should be asked every time a minister uses the reflection loop. Instead, use a few questions that seem relevant and appropriate for the particular ministry event.

Some Helpful *Identifying* Questions

What beliefs drove my actions? What beliefs should have driven my actions? Theological reflection requires identifying the theological themes that were at work and should have been at work in the ministry encounter. Compassion, giving of self, being a neighbor to all, and sacrificing for others are theological themes exemplified by the Good Samaritan in his ministry and absent from the priest's and Levite's responses.

What are the appropriate doctrinal themes that inform this ministry situation? Pete Ward identified a particular model of theological reflection as "testing," whereby the minister begins the conversation with certain theological assertions and then proceeds to test them in practice.[18] Ward's

---

18. Ward, *Introducing Practical Theology*, 104–6. Ward provides an example through the theological conviction of worship. If worship is a theological requirement and value for a local church, then what does worshiping actually *do* to the congregation? Ward is approaching reflection in this sense as a way of doing theology, but the flow he presents can be helpful for deploying theological reflection in the service of a specific ministry situation. This latter definition of reflection is, again, the approach of our book.

observation provides a starting point of *identifying* the theological theme(s) germane to the ministry situation at hand. This theme is then explored for pertinent questions, the asking and answering of which contribute to the theological reflection conversation.

For example, a church member approaches the minister for advice on dealing with an aged parent who desires to end her life through physician-assisted suicide. Theological themes and their attendant questions that could guide theological reflection would include:

- **Anthropological issues:** How does the fact that God created humans in his image affect this situation?
- **Issues about the sovereignty of God:** To what degree does God share with humans the power over life and death?
- **Sanctification and discipleship issues:** How can I most effectively express love to my parent?

While this is not an exhaustive list of the theological themes, we provide them to illustrate the general order or flow:

- Identify the heart of the matter.
- Identify the germane doctrinal themes.
- Then allow the chosen themes to dictate reflection questions.

To what degree was this a successful ministry encounter? What worked? What did not work so well? We do not know enough about the story to probe deeper here. Did the wounded traveler develop sepsis? Did he regain his strength? Were there other treatments the Samaritan had at his disposal but did not use?

What are my initial feelings based on what is going on? Ministers must pay attention to how their feelings affect how they react and respond to the ministry crises of others. Lack of self-reflection can result in great harm done at the hands of the minister. For example, feelings of unresolved frustration toward parents could negatively affect the counseling of a runaway teen and stoke the fires of rebellion.

What emotion does this stir from my past? Where have I experienced this before? What does this remind me of? What did I learn from my past experience? Past successes, failures, or missteps can be significant con-tributors to present ministry solutions. Every seasoned and successful minister has multiple stories of lessons learned that end with "I'll never do it that way again!"

Some Helpful *Aligning* Questions

The second step in the reflection loop is to work on closing the gap between our confessed and operational theology, theory, and emotions by aligning those issues we identified in the first step with our best understanding of God's truth. Again we take a three-pronged approach, comparing those issues to biblical theology (orthodoxy), understanding of effective ministry (orthopraxy), and emotional health (orthopathy).

In what ways can I better match what I did with what I believe and think? How do I wish I had responded? Identifying important theological and theoretical themes must produce an aligning process to ensure they are fully influencing our actions.

What are the issues? As obvious as this question seems to be, ministers still need to address it honestly. They must pray for wisdom as they ask and answer this question because the issues may not be what the stakeholders think they are. Given the perspectives and preconceptions of all involved parties, the real issues can be obscured and difficult to identify. Ministers need discernment and courage as they seek God to know the issues accurately.

Are there any blind spots? What is at risk? What assumptions am I making and why? We may operate under inaccurate racial, socioeconomic, personality-based, or historical assumptions, among others. The reality of a ministry situation can bring these assumptions to light. Wisdom, discernment, and courage are necessary to confront harmful assumptions.

Read between the lines: What has not been said? What didn't happen? As with a proper understanding of the issues and the necessary decon-struction of incorrect assumptions, reading "between the lines" can shed light on a ministry situation by forcing the minister to consider that which has not been spoken but rather implied. How does that data inform the situation and its desired solution?

The previous questions, involving issues, assumptions, and between-the-lines ideas, serve as good alignment checks. They force ministers to self-assess, making sure that we do not cloud the real issues of the situation with premature, unwarranted, or otherwise incorrect assumptions. Reading between the lines also forces ministers to approach a ministry situation from the angle of unspoken but implied considerations.

Did anything need to happen at all? The easiest course of action may be to do something—anything. But the best course of action may be to do nothing at all. As important as action is to the end of this reflection loop, the wrong action could be disastrous. Consider the possibility that doing nothing may be the best action to take.

How does what I was feeling correspond to my understanding of emotional health? While we cannot change how we felt, we can evaluate how emotionally healthy we were in the moment and make appropriate changes to become healthier. We also can work on lowering our reactivity and using appropriate filters in our ministry responses.

Did I consider the feelings of others in an understanding way? Being aware of what is happening with others is an important component of compassionate ministry.

Where is God at work? In what way is the Holy Spirit moving? Ministers must take seriously the possibility that God is doing something incompatible with their desired ministry solution. The Old Testament story of Job is a perfect example of God being at work in ways that Job's friends could not comprehend. Consequently, their solutions were misguided and did not bear fruit. Ministers must make sure that they are in accord with God.

Did someone try to control the experience with God talk? The book of Proverbs is filled with examples of smooth talkers whose words are actual traps (2:16; 7:5; 10:19; 18:8). Just because stakeholders in a ministry situation invoke the Lord's name or say all the right, proper, and popular spiritual words, it does not mean they are being truthful, objective, or godly. In fact, too much "God talk" may betray people's selfish desires to manipulate a ministry situation.

How could this end? This question relates to *possible* and *desirable* goals. In terms of possible goals, the range of projected options may run the gamut from highly desirable to unavoidably destructive. In terms of desirable goals, those options are the targets at which the minister should aim. Projecting possible ends will keep the minister from hitting nothing when constructing a ministry solution.

What were the reasons for performing this particular service or action? Asking this question requires honesty. What are the *real* reasons for doing this? Are they really *Christian* reasons? Stone and Duke asserted that Christians' reasons for particular actions typically boil down to two domains: "because of" and "in order to" reasons. "Because Jesus commanded that we love one another, we will . . ." "In order that the gospel may gain a good hearing, we will . . ."[19]

How will the desired response be consistent with the grace and truth modeled by Jesus? Based on the description of how Jesus manifested himself (John 1:14, 17), the attributes of grace and truth should come into play in the Christian minister's response to a given ministry situation.

Some Helpful *Exploring* Questions

The third step in the reflection loop is to *explore* possibilities for future ministry responses. It is premature to decide about what to do differently; in many ways, ministers can only make that decision during the next ministry encounter. Though we may encounter a situation like the present one, it will never be exactly the same. The next situation will involve different people, contexts, and cultures. If we have been faithful to the reflection process, we may even be more mature ministers. Because of those variables, we have chosen *explore* as the key word for the third step.

This step distinguishes the *reflection loop* from *doing theology*, which focuses on the Christian life. While we affirm the value of theological reflection as a means of living faithfully, the reflection loop produces theologically sound, effective, and emotionally healthy ministry practice. The reflection loop uses theological reflection to explore future possibilities for ministry.

Examples

Are there biblical stories or episodes from church history that are parallel to what happened in this ministry action? Questions like this one pull from the strength of the narrative theology–based model.

---

19. Howard W. Stone and James O. Duke, *How to Think Theologically* (Minneapolis: Fortress, 2006), 104.

How have I navigated similar situations in the past effectively? How have others ministered effectively under circumstances like these? What suggestions do respected authors make about how to minister in parallel cases? These questions use examples from the minister's past and circle of influence to explore how to minister more effectively in the future.

Options

Who are the winners and losers? What actions could lead to a win-win scenario? These questions point the minister beyond binary solutions of either/or, winner/loser. At first blush, particularly if a ministry situation is dramatic and pressing (for instance, a church lay leader arrested for illegal business practices), the solution options may appear quite binary, with the only questions being who will occupy the two roles of winner and loser. Yet if ministers take a step back, expand their perspective, and ask the "win-lose" questions above, a more redemptive solution may appear. Perhaps a win-win is possible. Perhaps the "winner" may share the spoils with the "loser." Perhaps the solution results in "redeemed-redeemed." To use another metaphor, these questions open up the possibility of gradation solutions on a gray scale rather than just black or white.

What is the most fitting course of action and why?[20] Ethical theories make a distinction between what is right and what is fitting.[21] Therefore, one version of this "fitting question" will emerge from ministers' desire to determine what is the most fitting expression of Christian faithfulness. But another version of the same general question could be this: What is the most fitting Christian outcome of this ministry situation? The answer to one question may be different than the other.

What deeds are Christians called to do? As the people of God, the body of Christ, the temple of the Holy Spirit, the people who pray, "Thy will, O Lord, be done," how is the church—including individual

---

20. Stone and Duke, *How to Think Theologically*, 104–8.

21. *"What is right?"* is a deontological response to the situation, based on obedience to a prescribed rule of behavior. For example, "It is right never to take a human life; therefore, I will not serve in the military." *"What is fitting?"* is known as a teleological approach, or performing some action based on its eventual outcome. "It is fitting to preserve and protect the democratic ideals of freedom; therefore, I will serve in the military." See, for example, Joe E. Trull and R. Robert Creech, *Ethics for Christian Ministry: Moral Formation for 21st-Century Leaders* (Grand Rapids: Baker Academic, 2017), 37ff.

Christians—called to act in response to the multiple ministry issues that surround it?[22]

Opportunities

How can we live Christianly in this situation? Ballard describes this question as an "existential moment," when the minister, and perhaps even the congregation, determine to respond to a ministry challenge in full commitment to God and his perceived will, regardless of the cost.[23]

What does God expect here? Robert Kinast maintains that asking this question is what renders the reflection process truly theological.[24] Ministers probably will not ask it if they do not possess a robust understanding of God's providence. At least some of the following ideas fuel this question: God is present, or could be, in the given situation.[25] God cares for the participants in the situation. God has a will regarding the outcome of the situation. God wants someone or some group to discern his will in a given situation.[26]

What principles, actions, or concepts are transferable? For instance, concepts that impact a ministry situation involving a person grieving the loss of a loved one could also apply to a situation involving extreme loss of other kinds, like losing a job, one's health, or a house to foreclosure.

CONCLUDING REMARKS

First, the minister should expect some haziness when practicing theological reflection.[27] We reflect in the service of ministering effectively in a specific ministry situation, which requires ministers to *identify*, *align*, and *explore*. But ministry is messy, whether we are beginning "in the middle of things," interacting with broken and hurting people, or dealing with

---

22. Stone and Duke, *How to Think Theologically*, 101.

23. Paul Ballard, "Reflections on Theological Reflection," *Modern Believing* 40, no. 3 (July 1999): 15. Ballard cites the phrase "existential moment" from James Poling and Donald Miller, *Foundations for a Practical Theology of Ministry* (Nashville: Abingdon, 1985), 88.

24. Robert L. Kinast, *Let Ministry Teach: A Guide to Theological Reflection* (Collegeville, MN: Order of St. Benedict, 1996), x.

25. Kinast, *Let Ministry Teach*, 20.

26. Paul Ballard, "Theological Reflection and Providence," *Practical Theology* 1, no. 3 (2009): 286.

27. Ward, *Introducing Practical Theology*, 114–15.

unanticipated yet life-changing results. This fog of ministry should be enough to caution all ministers that reflection never ends with thinking; it requires an appeal to God the Holy Spirit to guide and protect us as we respond, especially when the way forward seems ambiguous.

Second, the ministers' lives and ministries define the playing field of theological reflection. Even if ministers are new to formal theological reflection, they have already been engaged in it to some extent through their daily devotional practices and their relationship with God. In their devotional life, they have thought about God, read about and communicated with him, and submitted themselves to his will. In their daily walk with God, they have loved and served people, as well as having made good and difficult ethical decisions. All these incremental actions have a cumulative effect, preparing the disciple of Jesus not only to live well tomorrow but to minister *and reflect well* today. In the actual practice of ministry, theological reflection is nurtured. As Ward writes, "The key to developing theological reflection is found not in following a method but in the practice itself. . . . [It] cannot realistically be summoned out of the air."[28] Bottom line: As they live the disciple's life and care for people, ministers engage the fundamentals of effective theological reflection.

Third, we do theological reflection in the service of the church. Whether learning about theological reflection in a seminary or college course, employing a method for the first time in a new ministry, or augmenting a tried-and-true process with new ideas, ministers should remember that reflection is for the church. The body of Christ is both the recipient and beneficiary of the fruit of theological reflection (1 Cor. 12:12–27). This does not mean that Christians alone benefit from ministers' reflection and response. But it does mean that ministers undertake theological reflection, for the benefit of the nonbelieving world, on behalf of the church body in which they minister. Theological reflection in this case is an outreach and ministry of the local church to the world at large.[29]

---

28. Ward, *Introducing Practical Theology*, 115.
29. Ward, *Introducing Practical Theology*, 117.

SECTION 2

THE TOOLS OF

THEOLOGICAL

REFLECTION

This section provides an explanation of how to use the tools of theological reflection and includes examples of ministry artifacts. These artifacts, written by our research team and students, illustrate the ways ministers have used the reflection loop in practicing theological reflection.

CHAPTER 4

EXPERIENCING A 360° MINISTRY SUPPORT SYSTEM

At a Glance

- Community enhances theological reflection.
- Theological reflection is best done in a ministry support system that includes mentors, peers, and those served by the minister.
- Openness to feedback is necessary to maximize the effectiveness of the ministry support system.

THEOLOGICAL REFLECTION IN COMMUNITY

The disciples had a front row seat as the Son of God healed the sick, leprous, deaf, blind, lame, and demonized. When Jesus multiplied the loaves and fishes to feed thousands, they were there. They were in the boat when he calmed the stormy sea and when he walked on water. The disciples were eyewitnesses to everything.

Yet something was missing. They were seeing and hearing, but they did not understand what was happening right before their eyes.

Going Deep

Jesus's frustration with them was growing. In Mark's Gospel, it surfaced for the first time after they asked him to explain the parable of the sower and the soils. Before Jesus explained the parable he asked a question with an edge: "Don't you understand this parable? How then will you understand any parable?" (Mark 4:13).

Later, in an editorial comment, Mark said that they "were completely amazed, for they had not understood about the loaves; their hearts were hardened" (Mark 6:51–52).

Again, after hearing a brief parable about defilement, the disciples questioned Jesus about its meaning. Jesus became even more pointed: "'Are you so dull?' he asked. 'Don't you see that nothing that enters a person from the outside can defile them?'" (Mark 7:18).

Jesus's frustration escalated during a confrontation with the Pharisees, who were seeking a sign from heaven. As the disciples entered the boat, Jesus warned, "Be careful, watch out for the yeast of the Pharisees and that of Herod" (Mark 8:15). Since the disciples had forgotten to take bread along for their journey, they assumed he was talking about the lack of provisions and began discussing the matter.

As Jesus overheard their conversation, he asked them a number of questions in rapid-fire succession that were meant to rebuke them for their lack of spiritual awareness:

> "Why are you talking about having no bread? Do you still not see or understand? Are your hearts hardened? Do you have eyes but fail to see, and ears but fail to hear? And don't you remember? When I broke the five loaves for the five thousand, how many basketfuls of pieces did you pick up?"
>
> "Twelve," they replied.
>
> "And when I broke the seven loaves for the four thousand, how many basketfuls of pieces did you pick up?"
>
> They answered, "Seven."
>
> He said to them, "Do you still not understand?" (Mark 8:17–21)[1]

By warning them of the yeast of the Pharisees and Herod, Jesus was directing them into reflection, "but the disciples showed little interest in

---

1. "'Remembering,' together with perceiving, understanding, seeing, and hearing, is an essential part of the process of enlightenment in which they have been so conspicuously unsuccessful." R. T. France, *The Gospel of Mark: A Commentary on the Greek Text*, New International Greek Testament Commentary (Grand Rapids: Eerdmans, 2002), 317.

probing metaphors. They sidestepped the parabolic language and focused their mental powers on the literal facts: they had not brought any bread with them."[2]

Jesus's frustration with his disciples signals a pressing need for ministers to go beyond surface observations about life and ministry. He wanted them to go deep. In Mark's Gospel, Jesus did not reprimand the disciples for not believing;[3] the real problem was not seeing and understanding.[4] The danger of the hardened heart is not for those who do not believe; "an ignorant heart cannot harden itself."[5] The clear and present danger is for those who claim to have faith but refuse to do the hard work of perceiving. Kernaghan notes:

> This provocative sequence of questions was intended to bring them face to face with the problem of their hardened hearts. There was something here that they had to sort out for themselves, something they could learn only by coming to terms with it themselves. It was not a concept he could lecture about, a sermon he could preach or a proposition he could illustrate.[6]

Jesus expected the disciples to reflect theologically—they were to go beyond surface thinking into deeper reflection in order to encounter greater understanding. Reflection was necessary for the disciples to understand what was happening around them and what Jesus was teaching them.[7]

What if the disciples would have thought deeply about the fishes and the loaves and processed Jesus's words together, instead of being content with their surface observations? What would have happened if

---

2. Ronald J. Kernaghan, *Mark*, The IVP New Testament Commentary Series (Downers Grove, IL: InterVarsity Press, 2007), 150.

3. Although Matthew's account mentions that Jesus called them "you of little faith" (Matt. 16:8).

4. James R. Edwards, *The Gospel according to Mark*, Pillar New Testament Commentary (Grand Rapids: Eerdmans, 2002), 240.

5. Edwards, *Mark*, 240.

6. Kernaghan, *Mark*, 152.

7. Theological reflection is the ongoing process of theology as "faith seeking understanding." Daniel L. Migliore, *Faith Seeking Understanding: An Introduction to Christian Theology*, 2nd ed. (Grand Rapids: Eerdmans, 2004), 2.

they were not so self-absorbed about their failure to provide supplies for Jesus?[8]

Processing in Community

If they would have processed the events, using theological reflection, it might have sounded something like this:

Jesus enters into the boat and says, "Watch out! Beware of the leaven of the Pharisees and the leaven of Herod."

With Jesus out of earshot, Matthew says, "That's an odd thing to say. What do you think it means?"

"Maybe it's because we didn't bring any bread," says Thomas.

Peter replies, "I don't think so. He didn't say bread."

John asks, "Did you see how frustrated he seemed to be? What was happening before we got in the boat?"

Matthew recalls, "Well, he was arguing with the Pharisees. They were going on about a sign from heaven—as if every miracle he has already done hasn't been a sign. They are just refusing to see. They were hardening their hearts."

Nathaniel joins in, "It must be about that. I don't think it is about bread at all. Besides, we would not buy leaven from the Pharisees. They're not shopkeepers."

Thinking he is funny, Andrew says, "We do have one loaf here. If we get hungry he can just multiply it. It is not as if he has not done that before."

Unamused, Matthew says, "So what did he mean about leaven?"

"Well, what do we know about leaven?" asks James.

Philip answers, "It makes the bread rise. Just a tiny pinch soon influences the entire lump of dough."

"Leaven is supposed to be purged from the home for Passover," added the Zealot.

James the Younger gets into the discussion: "Why is that?"

---

8. Craig S. Keener, *The Gospel of Matthew: A Socio-Rhetorical Commentary* (Grand Rapids: Eerdmans, 2009), 422.

"A symbolism I assume," says Thaddeus. "Just as leaven spreads through the dough, evil can spread, so we get rid of the evil influences at Passover so we can have a fresh start afterward."

After a pause, Matthew says, "Maybe that is what this is all about. The leaven of the Pharisees is their teachings that can spread and infect as leaven does to dough. He is telling us to be on guard against the attitude and the teachings of the Pharisees."

"Ah," they all say together, "that's what he means."

In this fictional account, the disciples entered into theological reflection, looking for a path forward. They took into account emotions, setting, traditions, culture, and biblical teachings, so they could explore future possibilities.

The disciples would eventually learn to do this, especially after Pentecost brought the indwelling and empowerment of the Holy Spirit to the church at large. This is evidenced by Luke's account of the Jerusalem Council in Acts 15. At this gathering, they looked into the events unfolding before them that arose from the debate between Paul and Barnabas, on the one side, and those of the circumcision party, on the other. The issue at stake was monumental: must new believers among the gentiles be circumcised and keep the Jewish law to be saved?

Looking closely at the record in Acts, we see a testimony from Peter as the first to see gentile conversions as well as his theological summary. Barnabas and Paul gave witness to signs and wonders God had done through them among the gentiles. This served as tangible evidence of God at work. James related the entire matter to his understanding of the Scriptures and made a recommendation to help them move forward. They worked through this issue until they "all agreed" (Acts 15:25) and, by implication, spent time seeking an affirmation from the Spirit of God (Acts 15:28).

They did all of this in community. In this case, their reflection was during their ongoing ministry under Jesus's supervision. But reflection can also occur during formal training. Regardless, theological reflection thrives in community—a ministry support system where processing can occur and feedback flows.

A MINISTRY SUPPORT SYSTEM

Receiving feedback can be uncomfortable. Even when the feedback is accurate, it can be traumatic to hear.[9] How do you think the disciples felt when Jesus chastised them in Mark 8:17–21? We suspect Jesus got their attention.

Feedback can be especially difficult to hear when presented in a harsh way from an unloving source. In *The Art and Science of 360° Feedback*, Richard Lepsinger and Anntoinette Luicia write,

> In Walt Disney's *Snow White and the Seven Dwarfs*, the wicked queen self-confidently demands of her magic mirror, "Mirror, mirror on the wall, who's the fairest of them all?" When, to her horror, the mirror brusquely reveals that her beauty has been surpassed by Snow White's, the evil queen flies into a rage and plots her revenge. In our opinion, the mirror's manner of presenting the feedback had a great deal to do with the queen's reaction. While 360° feedback is a powerful tool—a mirror that reveals a manager's effectiveness from the various points of view of those he or she works with closely—like the truth-telling magic mirror, it may give us information we did not expect and do not want to hear.[10]

Receiving feedback from a ministry support team does not have to be a traumatic experience. If given and received in a loving, caring environment, feedback can benefit ministers by providing them with needed encouragement and information.

Feedback Provides Ministers with Needed Encouragement

Not all feedback is negative. Sometimes, it is a positive affirmation of a job well done. But if it is provided by a caring person who wants the best for the minister, then even when it contains criticism, it is a positive

---

9. William T. Pyle and Mary Alice Seals, eds., *Experiencing Ministry Supervision: A Field-Based Approach* (Nashville: B&H, 1995), 73. "Discovering from feedback the way in which others perceive your ministry may be traumatic."

10. Richard Lepsinger and Anntoinette D. Luicia. *The Art and Science of 360° Feedback* (San Francisco: Jossey-Bass, 1997), 143.

thing.[11] Peter certainly benefited from Paul's confrontation about his hypocritical behavior (Gal. 2:11-13). Feedback—negative and positive—is a part of true, biblical community.[12]

Feedback Provides Ministers with Needed Information

Ministers are not as good as their cheerleaders say, nor are they as bad as their critics insist. Without a formal feedback system, ministers are prone to believe one group and downplay the feedback of the other. Or worse yet, they will live inside their own heads without any outside perspective. Ministers need truthful, accurate information from people who are invested in their success—*cheerleading critics* if you will.

George Hillman writes, "Outside feedback is critical to get a reality check, no matter if it is related to health or to leadership development. We all have blind spots. Having a formal, structured means of feedback allows you the opportunity to pause and to assess your growth and your effectiveness."[13] With a reliable, healthy feedback team of truth tellers who care for them and have a stake in their success, ministers have accurate information to help them set their personal and professional improvement plans.

Those who resist criticism or feedback shut down an important tributary of information. Theological reflection thrives on information and flourishes in an environment with multiple feedback perspectives, including mentors, peers, and those whom ministers serve.[14]

---

11. George Hillman, ed., *Preparing for Ministry: A Practical Guide to Theological Field Education* (Grand Rapids: Kregel, 2008), 192. "Students do not need an exclusive diet of flattery, nor do they need to be told only what they are doing wrong or deficiently. They need critically helpful feedback from people who care about them and know what they are doing."

12. Hillman, *Preparing for Ministry*, 179. "Evaluating the feedback of others helps build biblical community."

13. George M. Hillman Jr., *Ministry Greenhouse: Cultivating Environments for Practical Learning* (Herndon, NC: Alban Institute, 2008), 94.

14. Richard Lepsinger and Anntoinette D. Luicia, *The Art and Science of 360° Feedback* (San Francisco: Jossey-Bass, 1997), 9: "360° Feedback: By gathering information from many different people, it provides a complete portrait of behavior on the job—one that looks at people from every angle and every perspective, in their roles as direct reports, team members, managers of both internal and external relationships, and sources of knowledge and expertise."

THE MEMBERS OF A MINISTRY SUPPORT TEAM

Mentors

One positive example of a mentoring relationship in Scripture is the apostle Paul and his young protégé Timothy. Writers of discipleship books often highlight this relationship as an example of a discipleship relationship. This has happened with such frequency that people often refer to a one-on-one discipleship strategy as a Paul and Timothy relationship. While Paul may have helped Timothy grow in his faith, the primary purpose of their relationship was to develop Timothy as a minister of the gospel. Paul was a ministry mentor to Timothy.

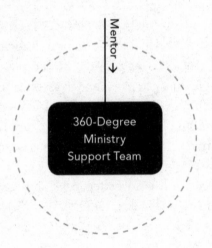

Mentoring Relationships Are Dynamic

Timothy probably came to faith in Christ under Paul's ministry (1 Cor. 4:17; 1 Tim. 1:2; 2 Tim. 1:2), during Paul's trip to Lystra (Acts 14:6) on his first ministry journey. It is likely that Timothy experienced persecution for his faith as a young convert (2 Tim. 3:10–11) and met with Paul on his second missionary journey through Lystra (Acts 16:1). Paul and Timothy's relationship began early in Paul's ministry and endured to the end (2 Tim. 4:9).

Paul and Timothy's relationship was dynamic, changing over time. As Timothy matured, Paul came to see him as a representative (1 Cor. 4:17; Phil. 2:19–23; 1 Thess. 3:2), a brother (Col. 1:1), a coworker (Acts 16:3), and a faithful son (Phil. 2:22).

Reflections ---

"By the last mentoring meeting, just days before graduation, I began to grasp the depth of change that had occurred in our relationship.

"Our connection had transformed from a simple 'master-apprentice' relationship into a mutually respectful peer-to-peer relationship. Our relationship had appropriately evolved over the course of time.

"As alone as I had felt at times, as hesitant as I had been in moments of confusion and lack of clarity, my mentor was with me. He remained a consistent presence.

"He was wise, without holding an attitude of superiority. He used guiding questions rather than feeling the need to constantly tell me what he thought I should do. My mentor was consistent. He was a realistic cheerleader. He was a coach and a guide. He was a friend."

Characteristics of a Good Mentor ---

- Good reputation and is respected by peers
- Has ministry experience that you desire to learn and practice
- Demonstrates a willingness to invest in you
- Is willing to listen to you
- Is trustworthy
- Will be willing to push and challenge you
- Has a good track record of working with people
- Desires to leave a legacy, not build a kingdom
- Is willing to invest the time to help you grow and develop

Mentors Facilitate Theological Reflection

Paul wrote, "Reflect on what I am saying, for the Lord will give you insight into all this" (2 Tim. 2:7). The Greek word translated *reflect* means "to direct one's mind to a subject," and in older Greek usage it had the sense of "to perceive" or "to notice" in the "sense of receiving both sensual and mental impressions."[15] The same word appeared in the Gospels when Jesus spoke pointedly to his disciples about not "perceiving."[16] They had failed to take in through their senses and mental processes what was taking place in their experience on a deeper "God" level. They were not reflecting on life through theological eyes.

"Considering" or "perceiving" can lead to life transformation as indicated in Romans 12:2 ("be transformed by the renewing of your mind") and Ephesians 4:23 ("to be made new in the attitude of your minds").

As Paul invited Timothy into theological reflection, he trusted God to be active in the process to bring insight and enlightenment.

> I keep asking that the God of our Lord Jesus Christ, the glorious Father, may give you the Spirit of wisdom and revelation, so that you may know him better. I pray that the eyes of your heart may be enlightened in order that you may know the hope to which he has called you, the riches of his glorious inheritance in his holy people, and his incomparably great power for us who believe. That power is the same as the mighty strength . . . (Eph. 1:17–19)

Mentors Encourage Their Mentees

Further insight into their mentoring relationship comes from examining the personal letters Paul wrote to Timothy. Through the years, young ministers have benefited from reading these letters because they contain instructions from an elder minister to his young protégé. In these letters we find the heart of their mentor-mentee relationship.

Paul wanted Timothy to succeed as a minister and serve God faithfully. Paul's letters provide instruction, guidance, and wisdom. The letters were personal, from his heart to Timothy. In one place, he told Timothy not to let anyone discount his ministry because of his young age (1 Tim. 4:12). Paul believed in Timothy and wanted him to minister with confidence. His first letter ended with an impassioned charge to Timothy to remain faithful in service (1 Tim. 6:11–21).

---

15. Gerhard Kittel, ed., *Theological Dictionary of the New Testament*, vol. 4, trans. and ed. Geoffrey W. Bromiley (Grand Rapids: Eerdmans, 1967), 948.
16. Matt. 15:17; 16:9, 11; Mark 7:18; 8:17.

Mentors Exhort Their Mentees

Just before his death, Paul wrote a second letter to Timothy, encouraging him to be faithful and to preach the Word. In the middle of that letter, Paul compared ministry to being a soldier who sought to please the commanding officer (2 Tim. 2:3–4), an athlete that competed faithfully according to the rules (2 Tim. 2:5), and a hardworking farmer who received a share of the crops (2 Tim. 2:6).

Paul's relationship with Timothy provides an example of what a positive mentor will do with a mentee. Notice what Paul did for Timothy:

- Prayed for him
- Encouraged him
- Helped him grow in his faith
- Held him accountable
- Instructed him in the ways of effective ministry
- Encouraged him to reflect
- Ministered with him
- Entered his life

Every mentoring relationship has the potential to be significant. My (Wilson) mentor when I was a seminary student did all those things with me. I owe him more than I could ever repay. Our relationship continued well past my student internship. He always seemed to show up on significant days in my life. On my final Sunday as a pastor before becoming a full-time professor, I looked up to see him in the audience. I was not surprised to see him, even though I knew it was an effort for him to be there. Being there was his way of blessing me once again.

I do not know if he ever fully comprehended what his time, instruction, and support meant to me. But I did get a chance to tell him. When I heard that his health was failing, I flew to see him before he died. The visit in his rest home was brief—he was not well at all. I held his hand and said, "Thank you for all you've done for me." He responded, "Oh Jim, I didn't do that much. You don't have to thank me."

"We both know you did," I said. Through the tears, I spoke my last words to him, "I love you," and heard him say his last words to me, "I love you too."

My mentor, Hugh Morgan, made a difference in my life.

When I asked him to be my mentor, it was just to meet the class requirement. Little did I know that he would be willing to love, confront, rebuke, pray, and help shape me into a better man and pastor. Brother Hugh had a knack of asking just the right question to get me to think more deeply. Looking back, I can see that he was leading me in reflecting about life and ministry theologically to align my ministry practice to what the Bible required of me. Mentors do that. They encourage their mentees to think.

At times, my mentor was a cheerleader, accountability partner, and friend. At other times, he was a sounding board for life and ministry. He was always available. He was kind and gracious, and yet he could be firm when I tried to dodge responsibility for my actions. I benefited from his experience, the biblical perspective he offered, and his listening ear.

He loved me. He believed in me.

I trusted him.

As seasoned ministry veterans, mentors provide an invaluable perspective to their mentees. They are a crucial part of the 360° feedback team.[17] While they may not be at the same place on the journey as their mentees, they have been on the trail longer and have a sense of what lies ahead. They provide downward, vertical feedback.

Another helpful feedback perspective is from those we serve.

Ministry Recipients

Ministers are members of the community of faith. Although our roles call for more outspoken and assertive involvement, that does not exclude us from receiving ministry from others as well. Ministers should participate in all of the "one another" commands of the New Testament, not only as agents but also as recipients. For example, ministers should not only build up others but be built up by them (Rom. 14:19; 1 Thess. 5:11). We should admonish others but also receive admonishment from them (Rom. 15:14; Col. 3:16). As Paul Tripp writes, "There is no indication in

---

17. Matthew Floding, ed., *Welcome to Theological Field Education* (Herndon, NC: Alban Institute, 2011), 99: "Look at your internship as a journey shared with a supervisor-mentor and a particular community of faith who offer particular gifts of hospitality, constructive feedback, and communal discernment about the mission of God."

the New Testament that the pastor is the exception to the rule of all that is said about the interconnectivity and necessary ministry of the body of Christ. What is true of the seemingly less significant members of the body is also true of the pastor. An intentional culture of pastoral separation and isolation is neither biblical nor spiritually healthy."[18]

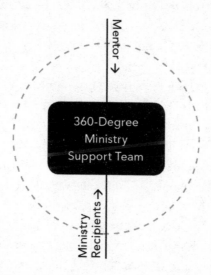

Reflections

"As a pastor of an Asian church, I expect respect from the congregation. Initially, I thought including church members in my feedback team was insane. However, my seminary mandated that I include them, so I did. Inviting six diverse members to join the committee was not the issue; listening to their honest and fact-based criticism was. It required humility.

"I am thankful that they were bold enough to confront me. Beyond just serving like a mirror to reflect the problems they observed, they selflessly helped and supported me as I became a better minister."

---

18. Paul David Tripp, *Dangerous Calling: Confronting the Unique Challenges of Pastoral Ministry* (Wheaton, IL: Crossway, 2012), 70.

In a passage addressing ministry leaders who serve as elders, Peter commanded the younger men to be subject to the elders and then immediately added, "All of you, clothe yourselves with humility toward one another, because, 'God opposes the proud but shows favor to the humble'" (1 Pet. 5:5). Karen Jobes comments that "arrogance, whether by domineering *presbyteroi* [elders] or by contemptuous *neteroi* [younger men], evokes God's opposition . . . humility in relationships is a paramount Christian virtue."[19] Humble ministry leaders will receive corrections and suggestions from those they serve.

Apollos embodied this humility in his response to Priscilla and Aquila in Ephesus (Acts 18:24–28). Apollos was "a learned man, with a thorough knowledge of the Scriptures" (v. 24). He "spoke with great fervor" (v. 25) and "boldly" (v. 26). Yet he had a gap in his knowledge, namely, "he knew only the baptism of John" (v. 25). So Priscilla and Aquila "invited him to their home and explained to him the way of God more adequately" (v. 26). Although the text does not explicitly say that Apollos accepted their instruction well, the acceptance is implied by the matter-of-fact account of their corrective ministry to him, by the fact that the Ephesian believers encouraged him to travel on to Achaia, and by Luke's report of his effective ministry in Achaia (vv. 26–28).

Vertical feedback from those we serve is helpful.[20] Another valuable perspective comes from peers who are on similar journeys and have comparable backgrounds. Ministry peers provide horizontal feedback that is often less intimidating and usually easier to receive.

Peers

Especially in the early days of ministry, some pastors find themselves serving alone. Others serve as a staff member of a church but experience isolation due to their function or age. Ministry can be lonely. For that reason among others, it is important to foster relationships with a handful of other ministers.

---

19. Karen H. Jobes, *1 Peter*, Baker Exegetical Commentary on New Testament (Grand Rapids: Baker Academic, 2005), 309.

20. Floding, *Welcome*, 97: "But as valuable as your personal feedback may be to the intern, there is much that the intern can learn by also receiving feedback from the laity of your congregation. Their perspectives richly supplement and reinforce the contributions you are making to the intern's ministerial formation."

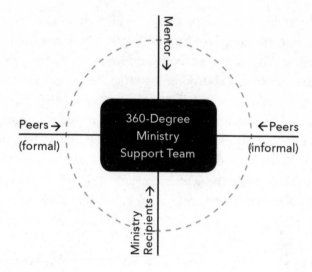

Peers Provide Essential Support

Ministers need other voices speaking into their lives and work. The essential nature of cultivating a collection of good voices—including voices of peers—can be seen in the following warning from Gordon and Gail MacDonald. They begin a list of four "warning signals" with "not listening to criticism from your wife, church elders, and others."[21] Certainly their advice to listen to your spouse and elders is important. But so is their advice to listen to others. Those they refer to as "others" could include a formal peer group. The MacDonalds warn that "callouses" can hinder a minister's willingness to allow people, even trusted ones, to say no.[22] Those callouses are byproducts of strong-willed leadership gone bad, prideful elevation of oneself over fellow church staff members, or even (falsely) humble self-deprecation that comes from serving as a solo pastor. Not gathering and listening to good voices can literally result in ministry self-destruction.

Like a well-functioning team, a good peer group is "a Christian environment" (brother-to-brother, sister-to-sister, and peer-to-peer) where both parties "question and challenge each other . . . with give

---

21. Gordon MacDonald and Gail MacDonald, "Restoring Your Soul," in *Refresh, Renew, Revive*, ed. H. B. London Jr. (Colorado Springs: Focus on the Family Publishing, 1996), 18.
22. MacDonald and MacDonald, "Restoring Your Soul," 18.

and take."[23] Such relationships require understanding, forgiveness, and respect for one another. Loyalty to one another allows both parties to "disagree agreeably," and respect infuses a sense of value and "high regard for the competency and ability" of the other.[24] The apostle Paul and the apostle Peter provide some insight into this type of relationship. Even after receiving a rooftop vision about accepting gentiles and participating in the Jerusalem Council affirming that gentiles did not have to become Jews to become Christians, the apostle Peter lapsed when he was with his Jewish colleagues and shunned the gentiles in their presence. Paul observed the discrepancy between Peter's confessed theology and his actions and called on him to align his ministry practice with his theology. Paul said,

> When Cephas came to Antioch, I opposed him to his face, because he stood condemned. For before certain men came from James, he used to eat with the Gentiles. But when they arrived, he began to draw back and separate himself from the Gentiles because he was afraid of those who belonged to the circumcision group. The other Jews joined him in his hypocrisy, so that by their hypocrisy even Barnabas was led astray. (Gal. 2:11–13)

In this case, it was a confrontation. Paul confronted Peter in a public place, demanding Peter live out what he said he believed. Sometimes sparks fly when iron sharpens iron (Prov. 27:17).

Peer groups do not need to be contentious, but they should be honest, authentic, earthy, and formative. The fruit from such relationships is wisdom for life and ministry, the kind of wisdom written about in Proverbs. A frequent catalyst for wisdom is the willingness to hear other voices. Derek Kidner notes several synonyms for wisdom, one being "instruction." "Correction/reproof" is often paired with instruction (Prov. 1:23; 3:11), thus affirming the need for perspectives and guidance from other people.

---

23. Dennis E. Williams, "Church Staff Relations," in David P. Gushee and Walter C. Jackson, eds., *Preparing for Christian Ministry: An Evangelical Approach* (Grand Rapids: Baker Books, 1996), 268. Williams writes about good church staff relations, noting several elements inherent to well-functioning teams. But these elements can also describe good peer relationships.

24. Williams, "Church Staff Relations," 270.

Kidner identifies another synonym for wisdom: "learning." This facet of wisdom also implies input from another person, perhaps a peer, whereby other angles and information previously unknown to the learner are considered.

According to Proverbs as analyzed by Kidner, wisdom is unattainable without the willingness to listen to others. One who is wise in his own eyes, or "calloused" to use MacDonald's analogy, "thinks he has arrived— and indeed he has, for he will never get a step further." Through "human advice and criticism" (see Prov. 13:10; 17:10), "the wise man is teachable to the end" (see Prov. 9:9).[25]

Ministers' willingness to allow other voices to speak into their lives constructs protective guards around their ministry and yields deep, fruitful, productive relationships. This vulnerability cultivates wisdom.

A peer group has a variety of purposes:

- **Safe Place.** The peer group creates a safe place to talk about ministry with others who have no stake in the outcome other than your safety and well-being.
- **Accountability.** As relationships within the group form, a member of the peer group might approach another member to become an accountability partner.
- **Theological Reflection.** Peer groups provide a perfect setting for using the reflection loop to examine verbatim reports or case studies.
- **Prayer partners.** When life or ministry becomes difficult, a peer group supports its members in prayer.
- **Problem solving.** Peers are often able to see opportunities in the obstacles we encounter in ministry. Their unique perspective helps solve problems that appear otherwise insurmountable.
- **Mutual encouragement.** Sometimes peers can help one another have a better perspective on life and ministry.

---

25. Derek Kidner, *Proverbs*, Tyndale Old Testament Commentaries (Downers Grove, IL: InterVarsity Press, 1964), 36–38.

Reflections

"Discussing actual life events and ministry situations was helpful. The camaraderie was real, and because of that we were freer to express ourselves in the safe peer-group environment.

"We benefited from everyone's uniqueness and from the freely given contributions that came from that uniqueness. Some people were able to contribute information, others resources, and others a perspective that was uniquely their own. All this together helped inform our learning experience and allowed everyone to be both a contributor and a recipient. This was a truly shared and sharing experience."

MINISTERS MUST BE OPEN TO FEEDBACK FROM THEIR MINISTRY SUPPORT TEAM

Because it is difficult to receive feedback, many people fail to listen and learn from it. Instead, they downplay what they hear by dismissing the person offering it. However, it is not wise to dismiss truth, regardless of its source. "From the lips of children and infants you, Lord, have called forth your praise" (Matt. 21:16). Likewise, from unlikely sources we may also receive, at least occasionally, accurate insights into our thinking, attitudes, and behaviors.

To benefit from feedback, you have to be ready to receive it like you would a gift, because that's exactly what it is—a gift from people who care about you enough to tell you the truth.[26] But like any gift, feedback does not always fit. You need to take time to evaluate what you are hearing.

Mentors, those you serve, and peers will provide feedback in a loving, healthy way to assist you in understanding their perceptions. But that is all they can do. They share their perceptions, which may or may not be accurate. Part of the reason it is important to have a 360° feedback team is so you can compare one perspective to the others.

---

26. Henry Cloud, *Boundaries for Leaders: Results, Relationships, and Being Ridiculously in Charge* (New York: HarperBusiness, 2013), 206: "To be the best you can be, you must develop a hunger for feedback and see it as one of the best gifts that you can get."

Feedback Metaphors

Feedback comes in different forms and serves different purposes. Some helpful metaphors to understand these forms and purposes are mirrors, snapshots, sounding boards, assayers, and patients.

Mirrors

Just as mirrors reflect people's appearances back to them, those on the ministry support team reflect their perceptions to the minister. Sometimes it takes courage to share otherwise private thoughts about ministers, but when shared in love, the information can be transformative.

Mirrors come in different qualities as determined by the number of coats of protective paint applied on the back, whether the backing is made of silver or aluminum, the amount of copper in the glass, and the thickness of the glass. Even the best mirrors have some distortion, but most modern mirrors give a fair, two-dimensional representation of what you look like at any given time.

Members of your ministry support team do not reflect your image back to you (like a mirror does), but they do reflect their perceptions of how you appear to them. Their descriptions are not an objective reality. They could be wrong. However, if mentors, peers, and those you serve all reflect the same thing to you, their feedback likely resembles reality and should be addressed.

Snapshots

Photographers on a cover shoot may spend hours or even days with a subject to get just the right image to put on their magazine. Why? Not every picture is flattering. Thinking of feedback as snapshots is helpful because it acknowledges that some ministry moments are more flattering than others. Support team members often will give you a "snapshot in time" evaluation of how the sermon or elders' meeting went—some will be flattering, and some will not, but the real-time feedback is invaluable for course correction.

Sounding Boards

The phrases "sounding board" or "bouncing an idea off a group" have become cliché. However, just as there are literal mirrors and snapshots, there are literal sounding boards. Before public address systems, speakers would often stand in front of hardwood backdrops to amplify their sound. Pianos and violins have a chamber with a sounding board, (a thin wooden surface) to amplify their sound. The function of sounding boards is to amplify what a speaker is saying.

As a metaphor for feedback, the sounding board functions to amplify the subtexts they are hearing and observing. As such, the support team is helping the minister to see more clearly what others are seeing; they amplify a subtle sound.

Assayers

Assayers examined the nuggets that miners brought to them to determine whether they contained gold. Because other minerals have an appearance like gold, it was important for the miners to get an opinion from an expert as to whether they had struck gold.

Most people have two kinds of ideas: good ideas and bad ideas. However, they are not always able to know the difference between the two. Rather than spending time, energy, and money chasing a bad idea, it is helpful to hear from an assayer if your idea isn't gold, if it is iron pyrite—fool's gold. Ministry support teams often serve as assayers who steer ministers in the right direction.

Patients

Before drilling, dentists often tell their patients, "Please raise your hand if I start hurting you and I'll provide more anesthetic." Of course, they don't want to hurt their patients, but they have no way of knowing what the patients are feeling without communication. Since patients can't talk with a dentist's hand in their mouths, dentists make sure their patients know how to communicate what they are feeling.

This is a helpful metaphor for feedback. It especially describes the relationship between ministry recipients and the minister. Unless a line of communication is open, ministers will never know what it feels like to be ministered to by them.

CHAPTER 5

EXPLORING GOD'S ACTIVITY AROUND ME

> **At a Glance**

- Journaling is rooted in church history and has theological significance.
- The journaling process helps ministers pay attention to God's activity in their lives and ministries.
- Ministers can structure the journal to facilitate spontaneous reflection while creating an artifact for future analysis.

People have been creating journals for thousands of years. In fact, there is evidence of Chinese journaling dating all the way back to the first century AD. In addition, Japanese ladies of the court kept "pillow books" as early as the tenth century. They would record their dreams and thoughts through images and poetry in these journals that they kept among wooden pillows in their bedrooms.[1] Journaling practices in western culture gained widespread popularity during the Renaissance era, with its cultural emphasis on human self-image. As the Enlightenment's Rene Descartes might put it, "I think, therefore I journal."

Some notable early journals include those penned by Leonardo da Vinci and Samuel Pepys. DaVinci's journals spanned roughly thirty years of reflection (1489–1519) and primarily contain paragraph and

---

1. See, for example, Sei Shōnagon, *The Pillow Book*, trans. Meredith McKinney (London: Penguin, 2007).

single-page entries written in almost illegible handwriting. The topics are wide ranging, including human anatomy, astronomy, poetry, color, sound, and the philosophy of painting—as you might expect from the original Renaissance man.[2]

Samuel Pepys (1633-1703), British politician and naval administrator, kept a journal over the course of nine years (1660–69). It contained reflections on current events, impressions of important people he met, and confessions of his sins. Pepys used his journal as a confessional tool to record his past sins and to reflect on how he could act differently in the future.

In the late 1960s, psychotherapist Ira Progoff began using journaling as a therapeutic tool because he discovered that his patients were much more honest about themselves in their journal writing than they were in face-to-face therapy sessions.[3] He developed a journal method called a "psychological notebook," utilizing a three-ring binder and multiple color-coded sections, which organized and systematized the writer's "life exploration and psychological healing."[4] Progoff's book *At a Journal Workshop* popularized his ideas in 1975.[5]

These examples reflect the nature of the practice of journaling. Sometimes they recorded random, concise, but significant thoughts (da Vinci). Other times the thoughts moved from purely descriptive to intro-spectively confessional (Pepys). Progoff's journaling featured intentional, focused self-reflection and deep contemplation.

All these historical uses apply to a theological context. Since journals contain an intentional written record of ministers' experiences, thoughts, and reflections, journaling is a spiritual discipline activity. The primary distinction of Christian spiritual journaling is that it is dialogical—that

2. Jean Paul Richter, preface to *The Notebooks of Leonardo DaVinci*, by Leonardo Da Vinci, vol. 1, trans. Jean Paul Richter (1888; Project Gutenberg, 2004), http://www.gutenberg.org/files/4998/4998–8.txt.

3. Jim Martin, "Journaling as a Spiritual Discipline," *Leaven* 2, no. 4, art. 8 (1992): 1, http://digitalcommons.pepperdine.edu/leaven/vol2/iss4/8.

4. Kathleen Adams, "The Development of Journal Writing for Well-Being," Center for Journal Therapy, https://journaltherapy.com/get-training/short-program-journal-to-the-self/journal-to-the-self/journal-writing-history/. Essay first appeared in *The Illustrated Encyclopedia of Mind-Body Medicine* (Rosen Group, 1999).

5. Ira Progoff, *At a Journal Workshop* (New York: Dialogue House Library, 1975).

is, an expression of our thoughts to God as well as a reflection of his Word to us.[6]

Journaling as a theological reflection tool builds upon a deep biblical and historical foundation. David's psalms and Jeremiah's laments contain honest, genuine self-evaluations and dialogues with God. The writings of Augustine (*Confessions*, AD 397–400), Julian of Norwich (*Revelations of Divine Love [Showings]*, late fourteenth century), and Blaise Pascal (*Pensées*, mid-seventeenth century) provide examples of multiple forms of prayer journaling.[7] Augustine's work could be seen as an example of "confessional contemplation," Julian's as "divine revelation" (though not in the sense of the phrase as it applies to the canon), and Pascal's as "meditative streaming."[8]

Puritans advocated for Christians to keep "daily short accounts with God" along the lines of physicians recording case studies and business owners auditing their finances.[9] John Bunyan's *Grace Abounding to the Chief of Sinners* and John Woolman's *The Journal of John Woolman* are part of the Puritan-influenced tradition of journal writing.

The Journal of John Wesley is a Christian classic. Jim Martin notes the famous entry of 24 January 1738: "I went to America, to convert the Indians; but oh! who shall convert me? Who, what is he that will deliver me from this evil heart of unbelief? I have a fair summer religion."[10]

THE VALUE OF WRITING A JOURNAL

Standing on the shoulders of those who wrote these honest, gritty, transparent reflections, ministers use journaling as a theological reflection tool to help them reflect on God's activity around them, inside of them, and to create a written record for future evaluation (see chap. 6).

---

6. Faye Chechowich writes, "In a journal written for this purpose, there are as many references to God and his Words as there are to our thoughts and feelings." Faye Chechowich, "Journaling as a Spiritual Discipline," Bible Gateway, 2014, https://www.biblegateway.com/resources/scripture-engagement/journaling-scripture/spiritual-discipline.

7. The Renovaré team, "Prayer Journaling: Styles and Examples," Renovaré, February 1, 2017, https://renovare.org/articles/prayer-journaling-styles-examples.

8. Renovaré, "Prayer Journaling."

9. Martin, "Journaling as a Spiritual Discipline," 1.

10. Quoted in Martin, "Journaling as a Spiritual Discipline," 2.

A written journal provides ministers with a record of what they have done, thought, believed, and felt over an extended period. The journal becomes a ministry artifact that can be used to identify and evaluate personal patterns, the discrepancy between aspirational and realized belief systems, and God's activities in ministers' lives.

It is a written document. While it takes much less effort to tell a story than to write one, to have an easily assessable record for future reference, nothing substitutes for a written journal. The journal can be conversational and does not have to be polished prose.

Because our oral stories tend to morph over time,[11] the words and phrases change as our memories fade. Once ministers record the stories in their journals, they have a more accurate written record. The journal entry becomes a reliable historical record—reliable, that is, to the degree it accurately recounts what happened.

Shows God's Activities around Us

We fill our days with family, work, and other obligations. All too often, we have more activities crammed into a tight schedule than can comfortably fit. When you add traffic congestion, spam emails, phone calls from solicitors, and the constant bombardment from social media, it is difficult to find a moment where our minds are unoccupied, much less time to reflect on God's activities. Journaling creates time in our schedule to record what took place during the day and to reflect on how God is working in and through us.

─────────────────── *Reflections* ───────────────────

"Journaling was especially helpful for me. I began journaling during a time when I was desperate to hear from God. I was feeling emptied of spiritual insight and new ideas. Journaling helped me process what was

─────────────────────

11. Kate Baggaley, "Your Memories Are Less Accurate than You Think," *Popular Science*, October 20, 2017, https://www.popsci.com/accurate-memories-from-eyewitnesses.

happening in and around me. I grew in my ability to self-reflect. Character growth and the discernment of God's will were fruits of journaling that led me to a new place as a Christian and leader.

"A few years later, God began calling me into a new role in ministry. I struggled and felt like I would abandon and disappoint the people I served. Even though it was no longer an educational requirement, I returned to journaling to help me process my observations and feelings so I could more clearly see God's hand. I gained confidence to move forward into the Father's call on my life.

"Even though I've graduated, I'm still journaling, especially when I struggle to understand a personal or ministry situation. Journaling continues to be the primary avenue for me to make sense of myself, ministry/life situations, and God."

Reveals How God Stretches, Challenges, Loves, and Grows Us

The journal becomes a reliable record of what happened, which allows future reflection on how God uses life's circumstances to shape us. Not all circumstances are pleasant. When they are not, the throbbing pain can prevent us from fully understanding how God is at work shaping us into the image of Christ (Rom. 8:29). In retrospect, ministers are able to revisit the difficult seasons of their lives and explore how God was using the pain to prepare them for the future. It was after introspection that Joseph was able to say, "You intended to harm me, but God intended it for good to accomplish what is now being done, the saving of many lives" (Gen. 50:20).

Prepares Us for Ministry and Life Moments

While case studies and verbatim reports (chap. 7) capture precise records of critical incidents in our ministries, journals provide a general summary of everything else. Not every ministry or life event demands deep reflection, but none of them is unimportant. They are worthy of spending some time in reflection, even if at a surface level. Who knows, the brief reflection at the end of each day may bear some significant fruit on one's life and ministry direction.

Gives Mentors a Feel for the Ministers' Life Rhythms

While journals are private documents, ministers do often share them with their mentors. After reading the journals, mentors can help ministers identify what is happening around them and clarify what is happening inside of them. With objective eyes, mentors are able to see ministers' blind spots and read between the lines of what is happening in their lives. The journal becomes a living record of what is happening in and around the minister and helps the mentor identify opportunities for mentees to better align their operational and confessed theology.

JOURNAL ENTRY DESCRIPTION

The ministry journal is a daily record that includes a description of the minister's devotional time, plans for their days, schedule, evaluation of their ministry, feelings about the day, and daily theological reflection.

Purpose

The ministry journal will assist in gaining insight into the routine of life in ministry. It aids in developing discipline within the planning of a day. It requires reflection on ministry and helps in understanding feelings that surface around ministry activities. It assists in developing intentional work habits and sensitivity of emotional responses in your experience. It supports the integration of theology and ministry into the practice of life.

What to Include

1. Entry number and date
2. Personal spiritual disciplines (prayer, Scripture, devotional description, etc.)
3. Daily goals
4. Schedule in two- or three-hour increments
5. Ministry disciplines performed (study, ministry activities, etc.)
6. Evaluations of ministry activities
7. Feelings about ministry activities
8. Theological reflection

Length

While lengths will vary according to stylistic preference, each day's entry will be approximately one to three pages. Evaluation and reflection on the journal should produce insight and suggestions for improvements.

Confidentiality

By their nature, journals are private. To protect the identity of others, use pseudonyms or initials.

Form and Format

While not a formal document, it is helpful to type the journal to make it easier to read and access. Each day's information should cover all the points listed above. The journal does not have to begin on any particular day of the week, but it should never skip days—even on vacation and days off.

JOURNAL SAMPLE:
Ordinary Day

Day 1—Wednesday, November 4, [year]
Personal Spiritual Disciplines

- Scripture and devotional time: John 14:16–18. Through the Holy Spirit God has come to be with me in my life. What a comforting thought! In this ministry to people in which I am involved, I am not alone. God is with me and working through me. I hope to always be an open and willing instrument.
- Prayer time: from my prayer list for Wednesday
- Spiritual discipline focus this week: fasting

Goals (What I Need to Accomplish)

- Work on preaching schedule for December
- Work on order of service for Sunday

▶

- Make a hospital call
- Work on layout for church directory with our office administrator
- Prepare for and lead church business meeting
- Visit one prospective member

Schedule of the Day (What Actually Happened)

06:00–07:30 a.m.	Awoke, prepared for the day, devotional time, and breakfast
07:30–08:30 a.m.	Drove to the hospital to make a presurgery visit to a member
08:30 a.m.–12:00 p.m.	Drove to church and worked on preaching schedule for Dec and order of service for Sunday
12:00–01:00 p.m.	Lunch with the chairperson of our stewardship committee (no church business)
01:00–03:00 p.m.	Answered email and received a call from a member in crisis
03:00–04:30 p.m.	Drove to prospect's home and made a good visit
04:30–05:00 p.m.	Organized materials for business meeting and met with our moderator
06:00–08:00 p.m.	Greeted people prior to the fellowship dinner and business meeting
08:00–10:00 p.m.	Home with family, watched TV
10:00–10:30 p.m.	Prayer time with wife before heading for bed

Ministry Disciplines Practiced Today
- Hospital visit
- Fellowship with a church leader at lunch and with congregation at dinner
- Difficult conversation with a church member
- Designed upcoming monthly preaching schedule

▶

- Created the order of service for Sunday morning
- Made a home visit to a prospective member
- Prepared materials for church business meeting

Evaluation of the Day:

A long but productive day with only one disappointing experience: good visit and prayer time with J. M. prior to his surgery, a major disappointment when B. D. called about his wife leaving him over his drinking, an encouraging home visit with a new family considering our church. I accomplished all but one of my goals—will reschedule to lay out the church directory. Reflecting back, I really believe that my preaching plan for October met the needs of a number of our people. I have received numerous encouraging comments on the series and am looking forward to sharing the birth of Jesus during the month of December. The fellowship dinner and business meeting went well tonight with a good spirit and closeness among those present. Dinner before business has really contributed to our fellowship and provided a cooperative spirit for the meeting to follow. Also, announcing the agenda on Sunday before the meeting has helped the discussion go more smoothly. Being able to see the written recommendations before Wednesday evening has resulted in less defensive attitudes during the meeting. I am glad John made that suggestion. I need to tell him that.

Feelings:

I felt I offered real ministry to J. M. and his wife during the visit prior to his surgery. J. M.'s faith in God is healthy, and I know he appreciated our time to pray. I felt happy and relieved to have my sermon schedule completed. I felt somewhat angry yet sorry for our member whose wife left him. B. D.'s drinking problem has resulted in abuse to his family. It may serve him right that they left him, and I feel much better about their safety, but I can't imagine how painful this must be for S. D. I feel helpless

▶

right now but must look for ways for our church to support her and the kids, as well as B. D. I feel the new prospect family will be joining us very soon. I enjoyed the fellowship of our people tonight and felt refreshed by their focus on our ministry task.

Theological Reflection:

Where is God in B. D.'s experience? Was he with B. D.'s family, giving them enough sense and courage to leave and protect themselves? Was God even a consideration when they married years ago? What is my role to B. D. and to his family now that they are separated? Can I be pastor to all of them? What does the Bible say about marriage, divorce, and mental illness when substance abuse is in the picture? These are all questions that do not have easy answers, but down in my heart I feel B. D.'s family did the right thing by leaving—at least for now.

Reflections

"I began journaling as a student, and it was a burden at first. However, the requirement became a respite by the end of the class. The discipline of theological reflection is one that I have grown to embrace and cherish. Had it not been for the educational requirement to journal for such an extended period, I would not have been able to see its benefits.

"Journaling gives structure to our response to Psalm 46:10, 'Be still and know that I am God.' Only after we are still can we reflect on how God is working and has worked through his Word. Journaling allows us to document the small whispers God reveals in the stillness of our time with him. Being able to recall these intimate conversations for future reference reassures us that God is in the unknown before us. While I do not journal as frequently as I did when it was required, I still value reflection and have found a more sustainable pace for journaling in my personal life."

JOURNAL SAMPLE:
Day Off

Day 10—Friday, November 13, [year]
Personal Spiritual Disciplines
- Scripture and devotional time: Acts 24:24–26. While the apostle Paul is under house arrest, Felix sends for him often to listen to him speak about matters of faith in Jesus. The power of God is on display through the spoken word as the text speaks of Felix being afraid, and he learns of righteousness, self-control, and the judgment to come.
- Prayer time: from my prayer list for Friday
- Spiritual discipline focus this week: reading Scripture

Goals (What I Need to Accomplish)
- This is my scheduled day off
- Sleep in a little longer
- Playing golf with three guys from church
- Clean up the recycle cardboard in the garage
- Dinner and a movie with my wife

Schedule of the Day (What Actually Happened)

07:00–08:30 a.m.	Awoke, prepared for the day, devotional time, and breakfast
08:30–09:30 a.m.	Drove to the golf course to meet the guys
09:30 a.m.–2:30 p.m.	Played eighteen holes of golf and had lunch with the guys
02:30–05:00 p.m.	Cleaned the garage and took a nap
05:00–10:00 p.m.	Went to dinner and a movie with my wife and went home
10:00–10:30 p.m.	Prayer time with wife before heading for bed

▶

Personal Disciplines Practiced Today
- Exercise and rest
- Break from email and the phone
- Spent time with some good friends
- Spent time with my wife

Evaluation of the Day

Golf is an interesting game and the ultimate metaphor for life. I have enjoyed playing for years, and there is something new in every round. The golf buddies I periodically play with have become good friends, and we are able to have deep conversation that normal life in ministry does not afford. The fellowship was rich. I was able to get the garage cleaned up, which delighted my wife. And our evening together was sweet, eating at her favorite restaurant. However, I picked the movie, and she would likely not have seen it without me. All in all, it was a fun and refreshing evening. And the late afternoon nap didn't hurt either.

Feelings

I feel energized to get back into the swing of a busy and fruitful weekend at church after a day like today. I am amazed to be a part of a great church, to have a few close friends to get some exercise with, and to share life with the woman I love.

Theological Reflection

God has created a rhythm to life with which we must get in step. Sabbath is likely the command that I break most often. Time and experience have taught me the absolute importance of taking time to pause, relax, rest, refuel, refresh. Hey, it must be important. It made a top ten list!

Reflections

"My journal revealed that what I believe (confessed theology) and what I do (operational theology) are often miles apart. My belief does not 'cost' me anything, but my actions do. It is calculating the costs that often cause me to fall short on acting on my beliefs. I need to learn to live out more of what I believe. While I recognize my deficiencies and the selfish (sinful) nature of my choices, I sense that God is patiently waiting as I learn to depend on him more.

"Journaling taught me some very important lessons:

1. I can be guilty of performing religious duties for the sake of appearance if it involves rote performance without connection to God. Journaling forced me to examine the 'why' behind the actions.
2. Spiritual growth is a gift (empowered and given by God) as well as a discipline (requiring endurance and perseverance).
3. I learned a better balance between thinking and doing.
4. I need to be purposeful in initiating and developing relationships. Life is meant to be done together.

"As a result of journaling, my activities have become more deliberate and reflective. I have begun to notice God's activity with greater clarity and responded in obedience to his call more readily. While the nature of the activity has not changed drastically, the meaningfulness and intentionality of the activity has."

JOURNAL SAMPLE:
Personal Crisis

Day 21—Wednesday, November 25, [year]
Personal Spiritual Disciplines
- Scripture and devotional time: Rom. 1:16–17. Am I ashamed of the gospel? It seems as though many times I live as though I am. I must be more intentional about connecting with people outside of church. There are about six people with whom I interact on a weekly basis. I need to learn their names, develop our relationship deeper, and be confident in what God desires to do through me.
- Prayer time: from my prayer list for Wednesday
- Spiritual discipline focus this week: evangelism

Goals (what I need to accomplish)
- Follow up with some visitors from Sunday
- Doctor appointment at 10:00 a.m.
- Lunch meeting with our youth ministry staff
- Final preparation for Wed night prayer meeting
- Email the treasurer and stewardship chair as we near the end of our budget year

Schedule of the Day (what actually happened)

06:00–07:30 a.m.	Awoke, prepared for the day, devotional time, and breakfast
07:30–09:30 a.m.	Drove to the church, checked email, prepared for prayer meeting
09:30–11:00 a.m.	Went to the hospital for my doctor appointment
11:00 a.m.	Spent the remainder of the day in the hospital

▶

Ministry Disciplines Practiced Today
- Plans for prayer meeting were made
- Responded to several emails from a variety of ministry partners, missionaries, and members

Evaluation of the Day

The day started as any normal day with one slight difference. I had a doctor appointment mid-morning. About three months ago, I received an email from my doctor asking me to make an appointment, and I did so for today. Upon arrival, the nurse took my vital signs and asked the reason for the appointment. I looked at her and said that I figured it was for a periodic physical exam or something and that I did not have an agenda but made the appointment as requested. She had nothing in my file about the visit but said that the doctor would arrive in a moment. The doctor could not recall why the appointment was made. So we began to talk about my general health. I shared that about two months ago I started having periodic breathing issues. Since the episodes were not painful, infrequent in occurrence, without a common cause, and I knew that this visit was scheduled, I chose to wait to talk to the doctor today. After telling the doctor all the details, she called cardiology, and I walked around the corner to take a stress test.

I was to get my heart rate to 144 during the fifteen-minute test. After reaching that in the thirteenth minute, the cardiologist determined that was sufficient, and I sat down while she reviewed the report. About sixty seconds after sitting down, I had a heart attack. My heart went into Atrial Fibrillation. The cardiologist called the ER folks, and within seconds about ten people went to work on me. After fifteen minutes of feverish activity and as things were calming down, I asked one of the nurses what was coming next for me. She said that she suspected surgery the next day. After an afternoon of tests, scans, EKGs, X-rays, ultrasounds, and other assorted activities, the head of cardiology

▶

came in to say that I had been scheduled for my quadruple bypass surgery at noon the next day and that the surgeon would stop by to visit me in about a half hour.

Feelings

Needless to say, I was relieved that my heart attack had taken place in the cardiologist's office. And I had to pass on that lunch with our youth ministry team and leading prayer meeting that evening. I am resting comfortably as I wait for surgery tomorrow afternoon. I feel quite confident in my medical care team. I know that my wife and kids are anxious, but I know I am in good hands.

Theological Reflection

Many times, we believe that we are indispensable to the ministry to which God has called us. That is the furthest thing from the truth. God does not need us. He can manage quite well on his own. However, he chooses to use us as he sees fit. The ministry staff at church managed quite well in my absence. It never was and never will be about me.

Additional Reflection a Month after Surgery

I made a follow-up visit with both my cardiologist and surgeon. I thanked them for their excellent work and let them know how much I appreciated the ways they have helped get me back on my feet. I told each of them that I mean no disrespect but that my life was never in their hands. God has given me life, he maintains my life, and when he sees fit, he will ultimately take my life. They were simply instruments in his hands. I think they understood.

JOURNAL DISCUSSIONS DURING MENTORING SESSIONS

During the timeframe that you are writing your journal, you and your mentor will likely exchange sections of it whenever you meet. Your mentor will probably provide your previous section along with some annotations, and you can then give your mentor the most recent journal section. Sometimes your mentor's notes will be the only feedback you will receive, but other times your mentor will want to lead you in a deeper theological reflection exercise using the reflection loop.

Journal entries contain mostly spontaneous theological reflections; they usually do not contain the kind of deep reflection necessary when using the reflection loop. You will do some of the deeper reflection as you read the collection of your journal entries.

The questions below are the types of questions that you can expect your mentor to ask you:

- Prejournal considerations
  - Have you kept a journal before?
  - If not, what are your thoughts as you approach this assignment?
  - Do you normally make to-do lists (goal setting) when you're not journaling?
  - How did you establish your goals for each day?
  - How did you determine the actual schedule for each day?
- Spiritual discipline considerations
  - Regarding the devotional reading, do you follow a Bible reading plan?
  - Tell me about your prayer list for each day of the week.
  - Tell me about your spiritual discipline focus. Where did that originate?
- Ministry discipline considerations
  - Which disciplines were outside your comfort zone?
  - Were there any new areas you were thrust into that you did not anticipate?
  - Are there ministry disciplines that should be explored further for additional training and experience?

- Feelings considerations
  - What feelings emerged when you compared your goals with what actually happened?
  - Did writing about your feelings each day put you more or less in touch with yourself?
  - Are you normally in touch with what you are feeling during ministry?
  - Are you aware of the perceived feelings of others during ministry?
  - Did you recognize any emotional triggers in yourself or others during the encounters of the day?
- Reflection considerations
  - Is reflecting theologically on the events of your day a new discipline?
  - Do you see any areas where you need to align your confessed theology (what you say) and your operational theology (what you do) in order to function out of a more deliberative theology?
  - Where was God at work in you or others over the course of the day?
  - Do any passages of Scripture come to mind as you reflect on your day?
- Postjournal considerations
  - What were the advantages of reflecting on your day in a written form?
  - What were the advantages of reflecting on your day with a mentor?
  - What did you learn about yourself from this journal experience?
  - Based on this experience, is journaling regularly or periodically something you would consider adding to your routine of spiritual disciplines?

In addition, your mentor may lead you into some deeper discussion with these three types of questions.

- **Accountability questions** hold the mentee accountable to their covenant, the academic requirements, and what they said they would do.
- **Clarifying questions** get information so they can better understand a situation.
- **Reflection questions** help the mentee reflect more deeply. These could be *identifying*, *aligning*, or *exploring* questions.

Accountability Questions

When mentors read the journal, they will pay attention to several things that help them prepare for the mentoring session. While not exhaustive, this checklist shows the kinds of things that your mentor will be paying attention to while reading your journal:

- Were the basic journaling requirements met? (Days journaled, content of the journaling process, etc.)
- Were the evaluations and theological reflections at a thoughtful level or just "surface" comments?
- How is the mentee dealing with emotions?
- How is the mentee dealing with stress?
- Are there areas in the mentee's life (family, health, sleep, spiritual growth, etc.) that he or she seems to be neglecting?
- What do I see when I "read between the lines"?
- Are there emerging trends (positive and negative) that need to be addressed?

Clarifying Questions

Because the journal is not a formal, edited, carefully worded document, some issues will need to be clarified. Mentors are usually pretty good at knowing what a mentee means with their informal writing, but sometimes there is enough confusion that they will ask clarifying questions. Other times mentors ask questions not because they need information but because they want the mentee to engage in deeper reflection.

Reflection Questions

While we do not have a full journal in this chapter, we do have three select days from a journal, which serve as an example of writing journal entries for an ordinary day, a day off, and a crisis-filled day. Even with these brief excerpts, a couple of issues emerge that would make for a rich mentoring session.

For instance, a mentor may say, "On November 4 you wrote, 'God is with me and working through me. I hope to always be an open and willing instrument.' When I read that, I thought about 1 Corinthians 3:9, which says, 'We are co-workers in God's service.' What does it mean to you that you are God's coworker? What does it mean for God to work through you?"

After listening to the mentee's explanation and asking appropriate follow-up questions to help the mentee fully explore what it means for God to work through us, the mentor could turn to the November 25 journal entry, and read it aloud:

> Additional reflection a month after surgery: I made a follow-up visit with both my cardiologist and surgeon. I thanked them for their excellent work and let them know how much I appreciated the ways they have helped get me back on my feet. I told each of them that I mean no disrespect but that my life was never in their hands. God has given me life, he maintains my life, and when he sees fit, he will ultimately take my life. They were simply instruments in his hands. I think they understood.

The mentor might say, "I notice that you told the doctors that they were 'simply instruments in God's hands.' Is that the same thing as being God's coworker or God working through a person?"

With this particular line of questioning, the mentor is probing to help the mentee think more deeply. The journal entry indicates that the mentee began the conversation with the doctors by saying, "I mean no disrespect," which would indicate that instead of seeing God work through the doctors to bring healing, the mentee was seeing the doctors' work as ancillary or secondary to God's work.

As the guided reflection conversation moves from identifying and aligning to exploring possibilities for future ministry responses, the two could brainstorm other ways to approach a similar conversation in the future. One possibility would be to say, "I want to thank you for allowing God to use your preparation, knowledge, and skills to save my life. I'm a bigger believer in God's providence than in random coincidence, and I can't think of a better place to have a heart attack than a doctor's office. Thank you for being available to God so he could use you to save my life."

Another line of questioning could be about the day off journal entry. The mentor could say, "I see that on November 13 you played golf with three guys from church, and on November 25 you wrote, 'I must be more intentional about connecting with people outside of church. There are about six people with whom I interact on a weekly basis. I need to learn their names, develop our relationship deeper, and be confident in what God desires to do through me.' I'm wondering; have you considered using your love for golf as an evangelism platform?"

In this case, the mentor is making a surface observation, and it may or may not lead to a fruitful discussion. Without reading multiple journal entries from the mentee's days off, it is impossible to see if the mentee's days off always feature socializing with church members (which may or may not be a legitimate day off activity) or if this was an anomaly. In other words, it is possible that three out of four times the mentee plays with a random group of four, and this day off was the exception.

A journal provides an artifact of the rhythm of life that is helpful for theological reflection. When you journal, you will do some spontaneous reflection each day, and some deeper theological reflection using the reflection loop with your mentor later. However, this artifact has another very important purpose, as we will see in the next chapter.

CHAPTER 6

FOSTERING INTENTIONALITY IN MINISTRY

At a Glance

- Ministers can analyze their journals to help them become more intentional, productive, faithful, and effective.
- The written journal is a valuable mentoring tool for theological reflection.

You will spend a significant amount of time recording your activities, thoughts, and spontaneous reflections in your ministry journal. The investment will pay off in several ways:

- The ministry journal has an immediate benefit in helping you notice God's activity in your life.
- It helps you organize your day.
- The ministry journal becomes a window into your life and ministry for your mentor so he or she can better understand you.
- You and your mentor will be able to use your ministry journal to do deep theological reflection using the reflection loop.
- You will use your journal as a ministry artifact so you can do a careful analysis of how you used your time and spent your energy.
- You will be able to see how your daily activities are working together to fulfill your life's purpose.

HOW ARE YOU USING YOUR TIME?

We have a limited amount of time in this life—only God knows how much we have (Job 14:5). While we do not know how long we will live, we do know that there are twenty-four hours in a day and seven days in a week. Those realities put a limit on how much time we can spend doing ministry activities.

If it were possible to minister twenty-four hours a day for seven days a week, then we still would be limited to 168 hours a week—and if we could work that many hours, we would still not be able to get everything done.

Of course, no one is capable of working 168 hours in a single week because everyone needs to set aside time for hygiene, sleep, relationships, relaxation, and down time. We have limited time to minister and remain physically, spiritually, and emotionally healthy.

The Lure of Technology

That doesn't mean that we don't try to squeeze more productivity out of our 168 hours. We try, but more often than not we fail. Richard Swenson gives a fascinating analysis on time and technology in his book *Margin*. He writes,

> The first mechanical clocks were alarms of sorts, introduced in the Western world during the 1200s. Only the bell indicated time. In the 1300s, the dial and hour hand were added. . . . By the 1600s, the minute and second hands were common. The invasion of the wristwatch began in 1865. . . . In 1879, Thomas Alva Edison produced the first electric light. If the clock broke up the day, the light bulb broke up the night. Humanity was flushed with the presumed victory over yet another of nature's limitations. Yet all victories have the associated costs. The clock and the light—they gifted us with time, then they stole it away.[1]

Swenson stopped his analysis with Edison's light bulb, but the technological attempts to extend our productive hours did not end there.

---

1. Richard A. Swenson. *Margin: Restoring Emotional, Physical, Financial, and Time Reserves to Overloaded Lives* (Colorado Springs: NavPress, 2004), 147.

Just as the light bulb extended daytime into the night, laptops, tablets, Wi-Fi-enabled cars, smartphones, and smartwatches extend work into places once reserved for rest, relaxation, and recreation. The promise was that these technological conveniences would enable us to get away from work because we are still connected. The reality is that they keep us from ever completely getting away, tethering us to our work and soaking up white spaces in our schedules. Technology may promise to free up our time, but it can take time away just as fast.

Before the smartphone, people averaged eighteen minutes a day on the phone. Today they are using their phones an average of three hours a day.[2] According to a Carleton University study, email occupies about one third of our workday.[3] Of course, there could be some overlap since people use smartphones for email, but even allowing for some overlap these numbers are staggering.

Could our attempts to save time through technology be backfiring on us?[4] I suspect technology will make you more of what you already are. If you are an intentional person, then you will harness technology to keep you focused and on your mission. If you are drifting, without a life-rudder, then you will spiral into a vortex of constant, meaningless activity and waste the most valuable commodity you have: time.

Reflections

"Because I kept a ministry journal, I was able to track how I use my time and evaluate its effectiveness. The journaling helped me to be intentional in how I use my time."

---

2. Eric Barker, "5 Science-Backed Ways to Break Your Phone Addiction," *The Week*, March 29, 2017, http://theweek.com/articles/688639/5-sciencebacked-ways-break-phone-addiction.

3. Steven Reid, "Carleton Study Finds People Spending a Third of Job Time on Email." https://newsroom.carleton.ca/archives/2017/04/20/carleton-study-finds-people-spending -third-job-time-email/.

4. Swenson, *Margin*, 15: "That our age might be described as painful comes as a discomforting surprise when we consider the many advantages we have over previous generations. Progress has given us unprecedented affluence, education, technology, and entertainment. We have comforts and conveniences other eras could only dream about. Yet somehow, we are not flourishing under the gifts of modernity as one would expect."

The Value of Intentionality

Writing to business executives, Peter Drucker says,

> One cannot rent, hire, buy, or otherwise obtain more time. The supply of time is totally inelastic. No matter how high the demand, the supply will not go up. . . . Moreover, time is totally perishable and cannot be stored. Yesterday's time is gone forever and will never come back. . . . Time is totally irreplaceable. . . . There is no substitute for time. . . . Everything requires time. It is the one truly universal condition. . . . Nothing else, perhaps, distinguishes effective executives as much as their tender loving care of time.[5]

Living an intentional life includes separating the important from the urgent. One helpful tool to separate the two is Stephen Covey's "Time Management Matrix."[6] In it, he classifies activities into four quadrants categorized by urgent/not urgent and important/not important.

After you have completed journaling for several months, you can go back through the journal and calculate the time you spent in each quadrant—doing urgent and important things as opposed to not urgent and not important things. Consider creating a customized and personalized time-management matrix and analyzing the results.

Reflections

"Journaling helped me realize how I could make better use of time. I analyzed the average time and percentage of time spent on various ministry activities as well as the average amount and quality of time I devoted to my family. The results showed I spent 50 percent of my waking hours in ministry activities, 12.5 percent with my family, and 37.5 percent on personal time and personal projects. Before completing the analysis,

---

5. Peter F. Drucker, *The Executive in Action* (New York: HarperBusiness, 1996), 550.
6. Stephen R. Covey, *The 7 Habits of Highly Effective People* (Coral Gables, FL: Mango, 2017), Kindle edition, 160.

I felt I was not spending enough time with my family and knew I needed to improve on that. The evaluation confirmed those feelings.

"Journaling showed my hunch was valid and helped me to make a course correction. I was satisfied with spending 50 percent of my time on ministry activities and did not change that ratio. The major change I made was to double the amount of my time spent with my family to 25 percent (versus 12.5 percent previously) and devoted the remaining 25 percent to my personal time and personal projects (versus 37.5 percent previously). Over the course of time, this adjustment has proven to be a good and significant change. I am a more reasonable person because of it, my relationships with my wife, children, and grandchild are fulfilling, and I am a better man of God."

You are responsible for using your time wisely. Paul wrote, "Make the best use of the time, because the days are evil" (Eph. 5:16 ESV). Before you can plan for the best use of your time, you need to take a look at the patterns of how you are currently using it. Drucker writes, "Effective executives . . . do not start with their tasks. They start with their time. . . . They start by finding out where their time actually goes. Then they attempt to manage their time and cut back unproductive demands on their time."[7]

Your ministry journal contains entries of how much time you have spent doing various activities, and if analyzed, you can gain valuable insight into what you consider a waste of time,[8] what you can delegate to others,[9] and what shifts in your schedule are needed in order to accomplish your priorities.[10]

---

7. Drucker, *The Executive in Action*, 549.

8. Drucker, *The Executive in Action*, 560: "Only constant efforts at managing time can prevent drifting [into wasting time]. Systematic time management is therefore the next step. One has to find the nonproductive, time-wasting activities and get rid of them if one possibly can."

9. Drucker, *The Executive in Action*, 561: "The next question is: 'Which of the activities on my time log could be done by somebody else just as well, if not better?'"

10. Covey, *7 Habits*, 149: "As a longtime student of this fascinating field, I am personally persuaded that the essence of the best thinking in the area of time management can be captured in a single phrase: *Organize and execute around priorities*."

Because time is precious, we have to make some choices about what we will prioritize and what will be left undone. After separating your activities into the quadrants of the "Time Management Matrix," compare the use of your time with your values. Are your values and your use of time aligned? If not, why not create a "time/energy portfolio" (see below), and invest your time in what matters most. While the work-life distribution of time is different for everyone, ministers typically work forty to fifty-five hours on the job. Some of those hours are fixed, some are on-call hours, and some are flex hours. Instead of dividing the day into hour-long increments, it is helpful to think of blocks of time divided by meals.

TIME/ENERGY PORTFOLIO

Sunday	Monday	Tuesday	Wednesday	Thursday	Friday	Saturday
breakfast, wake up, hygiene, exercise, quiet time, watch/read news, plan day						
Worship service(s)	administration, planning, staff mtg.	sermon prep	sermon prep	write sermon	family morning	day off
lunch with family	**lunch,** pastoral visits, appointment, run errands, take a walk				**lunch** with family	**lunch** with family
rest with family	appointments, administration, planning, counseling	sermon prep	sermon prep	continuing education	tie up loose ends, plan next week's schedule	day off
dinner with family						
evening off	evening off	appointment, counseling	evening off	small group	evening off	evening off unless wedding or other activity

The following example of a time/energy portfolio is for an introverted pastor who is a morning person:

Reflections

"In keeping a ministry journal, I was surprised to discover how I use my time. I saw a need to create a daily and weekly time chart to show how my time is spent on a weekly basis. Through this, I discovered that my time with family was the least I spent each week. I was shocked!

"Through the journaling process, some of the challenges to being a bivocational pastor came to light. My commitment to working forty hours a week in a secular job takes up a large portion of the week. For this reason, I needed to manage my limited time wisely. Being pressured by time constraints leads to an increased level of anxiety and stress. This was probably the cause for my desire to escape and become distracted easily. If it wasn't for the ministry journal, I would not have realized the mess I was in."

This example illustrates intentionality not only in its use of time but also in showing how to expend energy. This particular example takes into account normal church expectations and that the pastor is an introverted morning person, who intentionally allocates peak energy times for important activities and refuels throughout the day. Your time/energy portfolio will look quite different as you personalize a plan for you and your life demands.

HOW ARE YOU SPENDING YOUR ENERGY?

Energy management is as important, if not more important, than time management. If you do not have physical or mental energy to do something, designating time for it will not help. You have to have the time and energy.

Can You Identify What Drains and Increases Your Mental Energy Levels?

In common usage, introverts are shy, reserved, and perhaps even socially awkward people who reluctantly engage in conversations. On the other hand, extroverts are outgoing, winsome glad-handers who are the life of every party.

However, the two terms have a more precise usage in personality type studies. Personality theorists classify personality types by differentiating the ways people expend mental energy.[11] In simple terms, introverts tend to focus mental energy in their interior world (thinking, reflecting, writing, planning), while extroverts tend to focus mental energy in their exterior world (talking, interacting with groups, being around others).

Because it is often more socially acceptable to be an extrovert, some ministers have an adaptive personality of extroversion: They are masters at glad-handing and can engage in small talk with the best of them. They are the life of the party. However, their behavior is not indicative of their preference. They have adapted to their ministerial role. That does not mean that they are extroverts, just that they can function as an extrovert at an extreme cost to their mental energy.

On the other hand, some of what it takes to be a good minister will also drain the extroverts. Good sermons have hours of preparation behind them, forcing even the most extroverted minister to spend significant time in isolation. Sermon preparation will drain extroverts—preaching the sermon will charge them up. Introverts emerge from their study after preparing their sermon refreshed, but after preaching on Sunday, they have very little mental energy left over. Staff meetings with brainstorming discussion will give extroverts mental energy but drain introverts. Marriage counseling and committee meetings will drain introverts but charge extroverts.

You may be able to identify if you are an extrovert or introvert just by reading the descriptions above, but you will gain confirmation by taking the Myers-Briggs Type Indicator and processing the results with a certified practitioner.

---

11. Isabel B. Myers, *MBTI Manual: A Guide to the Development and Use of the Myers-Briggs Type Indicator*, 3rd ed. (Palo Alto, CA: Consulting Psychologists Press, 1998), 26: "To many laypeople, the term extraverted means sociable and introverted means shy. Jung's concept is different from and much broader than the layperson's view. Seen as different orientations of energy, a preference for Extraversion or Introversion identifies the direction in which a person's energies typically flow, outward or inward."

Do You Have Predictable Mental Energy Peaks and Lows?

Examining your time/energy portfolio, notice when you tend to do unurgent and unimportant activities. They are likely at low-energy times of your weekly energy cycle. Because you have no reserves to do deep thinking or interact with people, you migrate toward mindless, trivial activities. A better approach is to plan your activities around your energy cycle.

Monday morning for most pastors is not their most productive block of time due to the physical and mental fatigue generated from Sunday's activities. In the sample time/energy portfolio above, the introverted pastor has one recharging activity (administration or planning) with one draining activity (staff meeting) to make the best use of the low-energy time slot. The same pattern appears in the afternoon by mixing appointments with administration or planning activities. Unless a crisis emerges, Monday evening is off.

Because the pastor from the sample is a morning person, sermon preparation appears in Tuesday and Wednesday morning and afternoon blocks, and sermon writing is in the Thursday morning block. There may never be a week with this much uninterrupted time for sermon preparation and writing, but reserving it for that purpose allows for interruptions. If the pastor were an evening person, then the sermon preparation time would have included some evening hours, reserving this important task for prime time.

Do You Have Enough Margin in Your Life?

In the sample time/energy portfolio, we designated work hours with a shaded box and included a category descriptor of the typical kinds of activities the pastor will do in the block of time. The time blocks are flexible. The pastor can change them from week to week. But they represent an intentional effort to maintain a healthy work-life balance and a strategy to reserve significant time for the important activities like being with the family and sermon preparation.

The general rule of thumb is to reserve twelve to fifteen blocks for ministry or work related activities. This provides some flexibility in the event of a ministry crisis or a personal emergency. In the event of a crisis, everything shifts accordingly, but the intentional plan covers a typical week.

Notice that sermon preparation is in the first part of the week, and most of the time off is in the latter part of the week. This allows for some time cushion if a crisis occurs during the first part of the week. Then the pastor can minister to those involved in the crisis, and shift the important sermon preparation to the end of the week, taking less time off. The goal is to do important things before they become urgent. This is the same reason that family time is scheduled at the beginning and at the end of the week. By separating the time, it increases the likelihood that the pastor will not be canceling family time constantly.

Notice that Friday afternoon is for catch-up tasks—it is a flexible time reserved to do important tasks delayed by the urgent. This block is an attempt to build some margin into the pastor's schedule. In the same time slot, the pastor will also prepare a time/energy portfolio for the next week so that Monday morning can begin with a sense of purpose.

Another way to build margin into your day is to avoid scheduling a full day. Instead, schedule no more than six hours of work in a given day because the other two to four hours of work will find you. Keep some margin in your week and your day so that you can respond to needs as they arise.[12]

Are You Replenishing Your Energy?

There are things you can do to increase your physical energy levels throughout the day. Exercising—along with drinking enough water and getting enough sleep—is important to foster a healthy energy level during the day. Notice that the lunch break attaches visits, appointments, and errands with going to lunch. Of course, the pastor cannot do all of this in an hour, so this is an extended time away from the office, but by only leaving the office once, it saves time to attach these other activities to lunch.

---

12. Swenson, *Margin*, 13: "The conditions of modern-day living devour margin. If you are homeless, we direct you to a shelter. If you are penniless, we offer you food stamps. If you are breathless, we connect the oxygen. But if you are marginless, we give you one more thing to do. Marginless is being thirty minutes late to the doctor's office because you were twenty minutes late getting out of the hairdresser's because you were ten minutes late dropping the children off at school because the car ran out of gas two blocks from the gas station—and you forgot your purse. Margin, on the other hand, is having breath left at the top of the staircase, money left at the end of the month, and sanity left at the end of adolescence."

The box also encourages the pastor to take a walk at lunch. Getting the blood flowing throughout the day by taking a walk replenishes physical energy. Skip dessert; take a walk. Walking is not just for lunch breaks. Taking a ten-minute walk every hour will create physical energy throughout the day.

Pastors can schedule specific things in their time/energy portfolio to replenish their mental energy throughout the day. In *The Introvert Advantage*, Marti Olsen Laney writes, "Like a dam that harnesses the flow of a river in order to utilize its power, you should store up energy to spend extroverting."[13] The same is true for extroverts; they can store up their energy for introverting activities.

Look at the Thursday schedule again in the sample time/energy portfolio. Because this introverted pastor had a small group activity scheduled on Thursday night, the schedule calls for "continuing education" during the afternoon hours. The time spent in continuing education would help the pastor store up mental energy before going to an energy-draining activity—especially since it is at the end of the day and the end of the week. This intentional planning enables the introverted pastor to better function in the small-group setting.

An extrovert might need to prepare for an extended period of sermon preparation by preceding it with a staff meeting or luncheon with fellow pastors in the area. Know what drains you and what gives you energy, and make sure that you have sufficient energy for every important task, even the draining ones.

ARE YOU ACCOMPLISHING YOUR PURPOSE?

Are you spending your time and energy on activities that help you accomplish your life's purpose? Or to put it another way, are you fulfilling your calling? A careful look at Jesus's life shows that he spent his time and energy fulfilling his purpose.

Jesus lived with purpose. His mission galvanized his thoughts and directed his course. Sometimes he expressed it in grand, sweeping statements about the purpose of his coming:

---

13. Marti Olsen Laney, *The Introvert Advantage: How Quiet People Can Thrive in an Extrovert World* (New York: Workman, 2002), 167.

- "Let us go somewhere else—to the nearby villages—so I can preach there also. That is why I have come" (Mark 1:38).
- "For the Son of Man came to seek and to save the lost" (Luke 19:10).
- "For even the Son of Man did not come to be served, but to serve, and to give his life as a ransom for many" (Mark 10:45).

His self-sacrifice for the salvation of others was central to his purpose. "Just as Moses lifted up the snake in the wilderness, so the Son of Man must be lifted up, that everyone who believes may have eternal life in him" (John 3:14–15). It was necessary for Jesus; he felt compelled about it.[14] In the Synoptic Gospels, he repeatedly predicted his suffering, death, and resurrection. For example, Matthew 16:21 says, "From that time on Jesus began to explain to his disciples that he must go to Jerusalem and suffer many things at the hands of the elders, the chief priests and the teachers of the law, and that he must be killed and on the third day be raised to life."[15]

Luke's account of Jesus's transfiguration reveals the discussion between Jesus and Moses and Elijah. "They spoke about his departure, which he was about to bring to fulfillment at Jerusalem" (Luke 9:31). *Exodon* is the Greek word that was translated as "departure" in this verse. They could have talked about the exodus, the greatest salvation event of the Hebrew Scriptures. They could have spoken about the glorious *departure* that Elijah experienced, being taken up from the earth in a whirlwind in a chariot of fire drawn by horses of fire (2 Kings 2:11). Instead, they spoke about Jesus's departure, which he "was about to bring to fulfillment at Jerusalem."[16] Not surprisingly, the ministry travels of Jesus culminated with a purposeful final journey to Jerusalem. This phase of his ministry began at Luke 9:51: "As the time approached for him to be taken up to heaven, Jesus resolutely set out for Jerusalem." Why *must*

---

14. The word *must* in English translations of John 3:14 and Matthew 16:21 is from the Greek *dei*, a word related to necessity. See also Luke 24:26, where Jesus revealed that it was "necessary [Greek: *edei*] that the Christ should suffer" (ESV).

15. See also Mark 8:31; Luke 9:22.

16. Darrell L. Bock, *Luke 1:1–9:50*, Baker Exegetical Commentary on the New Testament (Grand Rapids: Baker, 1994), 869: "Fulfillment . . . is the key theme of this verse; the events discussed are part of God's plan, which will come to pass."

he go? Why was he resolute? Because suffering, death, and resurrection in Jerusalem were his divinely appointed destiny.[17]

Jesus freely subjugated his will to the will of the Father. He repeatedly spoke of himself as sent by God and twenty-three times referred to God as "the one who sent."[18] "Jesus is supremely the Father's emissary fulfilling the Father's will."[19] "'My food,' said Jesus, 'is to do the will of him who sent me and to finish his work'" (John 4:34). He expressed his sense of destiny with reference to his "hour," which ominously arrived when he perceived that his suffering and exaltation were near. "Jesus replied, 'The hour has come for the Son of Man to be glorified. Very truly I tell you, unless a kernel of wheat falls to the ground and dies, it remains only a single seed. But if it dies, it produces many seeds. . . . Now my soul is troubled, and what shall I say? "Father, save me from this hour"? No, it was for this very reason I came to this hour'" (John 12:23–24, 27). In the garden of Gethsemane, Jesus briefly explored the possibility of avoiding the terrible cup of suffering that awaited him, but he returned to his guiding conviction in submissive prayer: "Yet not as I will, but as you will" (Matt. 26:39).

The apostle Paul understood his ministry as a grace-gift from God. In response, he was vigorously intentional in seeking to fulfill it. Introducing himself to the Romans, Paul told them that "through [Christ] we received grace and apostleship to call all the Gentiles to the obedience that comes from faith for his name's sake" (Rom. 1:5). In using the phrase "received grace and apostleship," Paul means that he received the grace-gift of his apostolic ministry.[20] Klyne Snodgrass says, "At least fifteen of Paul's 101 uses of 'grace' refer to grace for ministry . . . the grace given to each person to do the work of one's calling."[21]

---

17. Joel B. Green notes that this verse, like Luke 9:31, speaks of fulfillment (somewhat obscured by the NIV translation, "the time approached"). Green, *The Gospel of Luke*, New International Commentary on the New Testament (Grand Rapids: Eerdmans, 1997), 403. Darrell L. Bock explains that the "Hebrew idiom 'to set one's face to go somewhere' indicates a determination to accomplish a task." Bock, *Luke 9:51–24:53*, Baker Exegetical Commentary on the New Testament (Grand Rapids: Baker, 1996), 968.

18. R. Alan Culpepper, *Anatomy of the Fourth Gospel: A Study in Literary Design* (Philadelphia: Fortress, 1983), 113.

19. Culpepper, *Anatomy of the Fourth Gospel*, 109.

20. Schreiner says, "The words 'grace' . . . and 'apostleship' . . . should be combined to refer to 'the gracious apostolate' . . . that Paul received" (Schreiner, *Romans*, 33). Moo says, "It is more likely that the second term explains the first: Paul has received the special gift of being an apostle" (Moo, *Romans*, 51).

21. Klyne Snodgrass, *Ephesians*, NIV Application Commentary (Grand Rapids: Zondervan,

Having received a divine commission, Paul considered himself "obligated" to the intended recipients of his ministry (Rom. 1:14). This was not a burden or drudgery to him; rather, he was "eager to preach the gospel" in Rome (Rom. 1:15) as he had "planned many times" to do (Rom. 1:13). Douglas Moo observes that the word for "planned" (*proethemyn*) "conveys a strong sense of intention."[22] When Paul returned to his missionary travel plans at the end of his letter, he gloried in what "Christ has accomplished through [him] in leading the Gentiles to obey God" (Rom. 15:18) and then hastened to testify that it "has always been [his] ambition to preach the gospel where Christ was not known" (Rom. 15:20). These statements illumine the remarkable intentionality in his missionary travels and apostolic labors. In Colossians 1:28–29, Paul summarized the intent and effort of his divinely enabled ministry: "[Christ] is the one we proclaim, admonishing and teaching everyone with all wisdom, so that we may present everyone fully mature in Christ. To this end I strenuously contend with all the energy Christ so powerfully works in me."

In Jesus's high priestly prayer, he prayed, "I have brought you glory on earth by finishing the work you gave me to do" (John 17:4). By praying this, he was not claiming that he had healed every sick person, cast out every demon, or fed all the hungry people. There was unfinished work, but Jesus had fulfilled his purpose—he had accomplished his specific calling.

Jesus knew his purpose. This is the first step of being intentional in ministry. You will never know what to say no to until you know what you are supposed to be doing. After you know your purpose, you can work to use your time and energy to accomplish that purpose.

God Has a Purpose for You

God had a purpose for Jeremiah prior to forming him in his mother's womb—he was to be a "prophet to the nations" (Jer. 1:5). God set the apostle Paul apart to preach to the gentiles (Gal. 1:15–16). God has a purpose for every believer. Paul wrote, "For it is by grace you have been saved,

---

1996). 200. For more on this theme of Paul's apostolic ministry as a grace-gift, see Thomas R. Schreiner, *Paul: Apostle of God's Glory in Christ: A Pauline Theology* (Downers Grove, IL: InterVarsity Press, 2001), 40–41.

22. Moo, *Romans*, 61n44.

through faith—and this is not from yourselves, it is the gift of God—not by works, so that no one can boast. For we are God's handiwork, created in Christ Jesus to do good works, which God prepared in advance for us to do" (Eph. 2:8–10). Just as God had a purpose for the prophet Jeremiah and the apostle Paul, he has a purpose for all who are saved by grace. He has works "prepared in advance for us to do" (Eph. 2:10).

No doubt, some of those "works" are related to ministry. The sum of what God has prepared for us to do is our purpose. Knowing your purpose contributes to your understanding of how to use your time and energy.

FINDING AND FULFILLING GOD'S PURPOSE FOR YOUR LIFE

In *Is God Calling Me?* Jeff Iorg defines a call as "a profound impression from God that establishes parameters for your life and can be altered only by a subsequent, superseding impression from God."[23] He distinguishes between three different calls:

- "a universal call to Christian service and growth"
- "a general call to ministry leadership"
- "a specific call to a ministry assignment"[24]

Iorg's first category affirms that God calls every believer to ministry. No one is exempt. However, God calls some from the community of believers to lead the others, those in Iorg's second category of call: "a general call to ministry leadership."

The second category of call plays out in different ways throughout a minister's lifetime. That necessitates the third category: "a specific call to a ministry assignment."

Only when you know your purpose can you know what ministry assignment is right for you. Your ministry assignment must be compatible with your call, your life's purpose. The following four principles will help you discern God's will about a specific ministry assignment:

---

23. Jeff Iorg, *Is God Calling Me? Answering the Question Every Leader Asks* (Nashville: B&H, 2008), 8.
24. Iorg, *Is God Calling Me?*, 30.

1. **The open door principle** (Acts 16:6–10). You can never accept an assignment that is not offered to you. If the door is not open, then you should not attempt to force it open.
2. **The singing heart principle** (Ps. 16:9). If God has made you for the assignment, then doing it will make your heart sing—it will bring you great joy.
3. **The blessing principle** (Acts 13). Your counselors, close friends, and family will see that you are made for the assignment and will give you their blessing. Sometimes they see it before you do.
4. **The Inner-peace principle** (John 16:33). God gives you a peace when you are in his will in general and will do so when you are in his will with a ministry assignment.[25]

While it is important to align your ministry assignment with your life's purpose, you also have to keep in mind that your life's purpose will always be bigger than your ministry assignment. Commenting on Billy Graham's influence, Pastor Rick Warren says,

> I learned from Graham to never lose your single focus. His focus was always on bringing people to Christ. I remember when Graham received the Congressional Gold Medal in the rotunda of the US Capitol in 1996. There were about 400 chairs, packed with VIPs. President Clinton and leaders of the House and Senate addressed the crowd, honoring Graham's life and achievements.
>
> What do you think Graham did when it came time for him to get up to speak? He spent maybe three minutes acknowledging the honor and how little he deserved it. Then he said, "Let me tell you about Jesus." Even though the entire event was about him, he turned the meeting toward his lifetime central focus: Jesus.[26]

A day is twenty-four hours, a week is seven days, and a year is fifty-two weeks. What is a lifetime? It is not defined by the number of ticks

---

25. Jim L. Wilson, *Pastoral Ministry in the Real World: Loving, Teaching, and Leading God's People*, 2nd ed. (Bellingham, WA: Lexham, 2018), 23–24.
26. Rick Warren, "What I Learned from Billy," *Christianity Today*, February 21, 2018, https://www.christianitytoday.com /ct/2018/billy-graham/rick-warren-what-i-learned-from -billy-graham.html.

on a clock but by an accumulation of choices—some are big, but most are small. Each choice may seem inconsequential, but when combined, they take on monumental significance. A life well-lived depends most on whether those choices align with God's purpose for us.

Your ministry journal is a valuable artifact that can aid in deep theological reflection and help you analyze your use of time and energy. It may even help you deepen your sense of God's call and clarify your purpose! There are other ministry artifacts that capture a "slice of life and ministry" that are helpful too, like verbatim reports and case studies.

CHAPTER 7

EXAMINING PAST MINISTRY, PREPARING FOR FUTURE OPPORTUNITIES

At a Glance

- Ministry actions can become ministry artifacts in several different forms, including case studies, verbatim reports, and a hybrid approach.
- Ministry artifacts are useful for personal reflection, discussion with a mentor, or a peer group.

We can learn from reading books, listening to wise teachers, and from listening to other people talk about their life and ministry. Using the reflection loop, we can also learn from our own ministry experiences. However, to be able to reflect well individually or with groups, the minister involved in the events needs to write them down. While there are alternative ways, such as role playing[1] and video,[2] to create a record

---

1. Role playing provides a platform upon which members of the group may play out the various roles in a story. With limited background information and only enough of the story to get the conversation started, individuals play off of the cues received from their counterparts playing the other roles. Discussion multiplies by dividing a larger group into smaller groups with each provided with the same basic information. Each small group would have time to go over the details provided and decide their strategy and direction. With enough latitude given within the limitation of story detail, each small group would have the opportunity to go in a variety of directions. A large group debrief in the end allows members to compare and contrast emerging issues surfaced during the various role play scenarios. The advantage of a role-playing event is that it allows for the creativity of individuals to move each small group in its own direction, thus allowing for a variety of discussion issues to surface. However, the disadvantages of a role-playing event are that it may result in providing less direction for the leader of the group and lost time to issues of less consequence.

2. Video clips provide a segment of a larger story to unfold in another dramatic encounter.

of a ministry event, the two most important are case studies and verbatim reports.

CASE STUDIES

Case studies are summaries of multiple ministry episodes conducted over an extended period of time that allow patterns of attitudes, reactivity, and ministry responses to emerge.

Writing a Case Study

Case studies should include four sections:

1. **Orientation.** Give the pertinent background information that will help the reader understand the context of the events and people involved.
2. **Report.** Tell the story. Give adequate details so the reader knows what happened, but not so many that the story loses focus. That you were wearing a dark blue shirt on one day and a white shirt on another is probably not germane. Report, but don't include commentary or an interpretation in this section. Allow the readers to form their own opinions before you provide yours.
3. **Identify.** What are the key issues? What conclusions have you reached as you have reflected on the event? What are you still unsure about? What is open-ended for you?
4. **Clarify.** What assistance do you want from your mentor or peer group as they unpack the case study with you?

Case Study: Senior Adults in a College Town Church
Orientation

Founded in the 1960s, University Community Church outgrew its first property and developed a new site with a 30,000-square-foot facility

---

This experience leans heavily upon the leader to scout out potential clips worthy to serve the intended learning outcome for the experience. After careful selection of an appropriate clip, the leader would need to prepare discussion questions in advance of the group experience. The pros of using video clips include a more professional ready-made presentation and the opportunity for a more focused look at a desired scenario or topic. The cons of a video clip include the need for more prep time from the leader and limitation to a preset topic unrelated to the broader subject.

and an auditorium seating 400. The city has long been defined by the university. Although the church's membership featured a diverse cross section of ages, a significant portion of the congregation was made up of faculty, staff, and students. In addition to a long-standing commitment to minister to university students under the direction of a full-time collegiate minister, the church also established a positive reputation as a church for families, with excellent children's ministry and an active youth program also led by a full-time staff member. The church also had a retired pastor on staff (for minimal compensation) to lead a ministry to senior adults. He and his wife won the hearts of many in the university town with their regular fellowship events, solid Bible teaching, and attentive pastoral care.

Report

I arrived in the mid-1990s. The pastor search committee told me the church wanted me to enhance the church's evangelistic effectiveness and spark growth. As many pastors during this time were doing, I promoted an attractional model, which included a change in the worship music to include more praise songs and the use of drums and guitars played more loudly than before. My main rationale for these changes was the observation that 64 percent of the city's population was between eighteen and twenty-nine and that the younger adults would more likely respond well to these innovations. However, the senior adults expressed frustration with the changes.

But the seeker-sensitive approach wasn't the only thing they didn't like. They also expressed displeasure at my lack of pastoral attention to them. I did not think this was a fair criticism and argued that the seniors needed to adjust their expectations regarding the extent of my personal attention to them. The church had hired Pastor Nelson (not his real name), the senior adult pastor, to care for their needs. However, Pastor Nelson tended to side with the senior adults, feeling that I should give them more attention than I was.

When Sunday worship attendance grew to the point that we needed two services, I saw the second service as an opportunity to address the senior adults' discontentment and unhappiness over the church's style of worship music. I felt led by the Lord to propose an early worship service that was somewhat more traditional and a later worship service that was perhaps even more contemporary. When I approached Pastor Nelson about the idea,

I highlighted my desire to provide a worship service that the senior adults would prefer while also enabling further growth in attendance. I explained that this plan would call for the senior adults to attend worship first and then attend their Sunday school class. The times would be the same, but in reverse order. Pastor Nelson responded, "You mean you're going to make us change our schedule? We've always had Sunday school first, then worship."

I explained that I was not forcing anything—just proposing—and sought to reiterate the rationale. Yes, the senior adults would change the *order* of their Sunday morning experience, but the worship music would be more to their liking. Since the church was seeking to enhance its outreach to unsaved university students, it was important to schedule the worship service designed for them at the later time, since many of them are up late and sleep in more. "So we'll have to go to the smaller worship service and won't get to be in church with all the college kids?" Pastor Nelson protested.

And so it went. Pastor Nelson was not at all willing to endorse and promote the plan to the senior adults. In the end, the church went to two worship services (both with a louder, more contemporary style than the senior adults preferred) and reached more university students and younger families.

Identify

The key issue I want to address in this case study is my relationship with the senior adults, which continued to suffer during my pastorate.

- Was I derelict in my pastoral duty to the seniors, or were my actions justified because I assigned a pastor to care for them?
- What was at the heart of my delegation of their care? Could it be that I valued the young more than I valued the old?
- Would it have been wiser to prioritize those who paid my salary? (Established, older, more mature believers often give more in tithes and offerings than money-strapped, young college students do.) Would that make me a hireling? Is this a false dichotomy? Is it possible to value both groups while prioritizing outreach to a target group?
- What was the conflict really about? Was it switching the order of Bible study and worship, or was it that they felt devalued?

- Was it right to call on the more mature believers to compromise their preferences for the sake of outreach to a younger generation, or should I have worked harder to train the younger generation to respect and value what the older generation needed?
- Should I have shown more grace to the seniors? Or should I have been a bolder, prophetic truth teller to them?
- The church grew. My relationships suffered. Was this period of my ministry more of a success or a failure?

Clarify

In summary, I came to perceive a tension between pastoral care of the existing flock and the missional mandate to reach new sheep. How does one strike that balance or know when to prioritize one over the other when they seem to be in conflict? What is God's assessment of this? What would Jesus Christ do in a similar situation?

Reflections

"Recording my life and ministry experiences and then reflecting on them gave me great insight into the strengths and weaknesses of the theological basis of my actions. There were times that I realized I had applied Scripture well, which in turn served as a foundation for future experiences. Even more often, I discovered holes in the theological basis for what I said or did. The value of discovering this was finding ways to respond to similar experiences in an integrated means where biblical truths serve as a motivation for my actions."

VERBATIM REPORTS

While case studies are helpful to reflect on ongoing issues, verbatim reports are useful to reflect on an isolated ministry event. Verbatim reports are detailed summaries of isolated ministry events, which contain some word-for-word dialogue of the ministry action.

When a significant ministry event happens, it is natural for ministers to talk with other ministers to share and get another perspective. Sometimes this happens over a quick phone call, a lingering conversation over coffee, or during an extended round of golf. Most of the time, the ministry event is one of many topics of conversation, competing for attention with other ministry and life experiences. Those listening are more likely to share opinions than ask identifying, aligning, or exploring questions (chap. 3). While some theological reflection happens in those conversations, it lacks precision, clarity, and focus.

In class, students tend to write down important components of a lecture that they suspect will be on a final exam. If it is important, we write it down. Employees put the date and time of their annual review on their calendar so they will be on time for the meeting. If it is important, we write it down. Most people make out a will after having children so they can designate a guardian if something happens to them. As they age, they revise the will to provide direction for the final distribution of their assets. If it is important, we write it down. Have you ever forgotten something at the store because you didn't make out a shopping list? If it is important, we write it down.

We write out a verbatim report because the ministry event was significant. It was important, so we write it down.

But there is more to it than that. Something significant happens when we take time to write about the ministry event. The act of writing down the event forces introspection, which produces "aha!" moments. Thoughts we may have never considered rise to the surface. The act of writing helps us process what happened.

The depth of theological reflection improves with a ministry artifact. The verbatim report helps those who read it focus on what happened. They are able to read important passages multiple times to see the nuances.[3] It is a far different experience to process a verbatim report in a peer group or with a mentor than it is to give a summary of the events while holding a driver at the ninth tee box and receive feedback in the golf cart on the way to your second shot. With a verbatim report, the ministry

---

3. Lee Carol, "The Forming Work of Congregations," in *Welcome to Theological Field Education*, ed. Matthew Floding (Herndon, NC: Alban Institute, 2011), 99: "If you are seeking feedback on a pastoral encounter or critical incident, prepare for such meetings by writing out and distributing your reports of critical incidents to team members in advance."

event is the primary focus. The recounting does not compete with other stories and become just another topic of conversation alongside sports, family, church, and life in general.

Reflections

"Writing verbatim reports allowed me to think through the ministry event. What really happened? What did I do right or wrong? What assurance did I have that I made the right response? Thinking about these things is helpful, but writing about the experience added another dimension in learning for me. In fact, after writing several verbatim reports, I was reminded of things I should do and things I should not do regarding future ministry. For me, writing my ministry experience gave clarity to organizing my actions with coherence."

Writing a Verbatim Report

When writing a verbatim report, following these steps will allow readers to investigate an experience involving multifaceted issues.

1. **Action.** What is going on?
   a. What are the facts? What is the background? Describe with adequate detail to give the reader a sense of the story's characters and setting.
   b. What was the crucial portion of the conversation? Write this portion in verbatim form. Present the dialogue that includes the primary substance and focal point of the situation presented.
   c. What are the issues? Focus on the crux of the problem, concern, challenge, or need in the ministry event. In one sentence, summarize what you see as the primary issue.
2. **Reflection.** Why is it going on? What should be going on?
   a. How would you evaluate the situation? Where do the key players stand regarding the primary issue? What's at stake for each of the parties involved?

    b. How and what do you feel in your role? What feelings are being expressed by others? Does this action threaten any values?

    c. Where have I experienced this before? How did I respond? Should I be consistent with my past behavior?

    d. What is the contemporary theological meaning? Where does God stand on this? What does the Bible say on this issue? What are the implications for the church?

3. **Action.** What are you going to do?

    a. What will this action cost? What are the ramifications or consequences?

    b. What are the expected results? What do you hope will happen?

    c. What ultimately happened?

    d. How will people remember the story?[4]

Below is an example of a verbatim report.

Background Information

This verbatim is a hospital visit I (Chaplain Ron Rinaldi) made with Mary (not her real name), the sister of a patient with whom I have a working history. The patient was a genuinely sweet lady in her early 50s who was journeying into eternity at the medical center. She is a Christian, and her family is devout. Her younger sister, the center of this visit, is close to the patient in age. The dynamic of this visit stemmed from the passing of their mother last October, which lingered on her mind (and the entire family present). The mother had a "difficult" death and appeared to struggle for hours, as I understood from the conversation. The family was not only dealing with the grief of losing another family member so soon but were also afraid to relive the trauma of a few months earlier. I was only able to speak with the patient on the first day of my visit. After her chemo treatment, she never regained consciousness and passed away five days later at the hospital. I had recently moved back as ward chaplain for the intensive care unit (ICU) where this patient was

---

4. Adapted and expanded from notes recorded by Glenn Prescott while attending the EATFE Biennial Conference of a lecture given by Kenneth L. Swetland, Senior Professor of Ministry, Gordon-Conwell Theological Seminary, 2012.

located at the time of my family visitations. However, this visit started as a sort of "divine appointment" as the sister and I crossed paths near the elevators. We moved our conversation to the small chapel not long after we started conversing.

We discussed many issues during this visit, but this interaction was the most significant part of our engagement:

The Visit

RON: "Hi! I was just headed out after visiting with your family. How are things going with you?"

MARY: "I'm holding up well." Her eyes told a different story. "Well as can be."

RON: "I understand—this is such a difficult situation for all of you. Your sister is such a wonderful lady."

MARY: "The family is meeting with the doctors at 2:00 p.m. to make a final determination on her care. Could you attend with us? It will be in the ICU conference room." We were in the hall near the elevators at this time.

RON: "Thank you for considering me to be part of this, and I think I can. I had one thing this afternoon, but I think I can work around it. . . . Yes. I'll be there. Do you know where this is going to go? What do they think at this point?"

MARY: She begins to cry. "You know we lost my mom back in October, and I remember how hard that was." In addition to grief, I sensed some fear. "She died at home under the care of the hospital, but I was the one giving her the medication. I called them over and over again and said we needed more medication. They promised it would be fast, but it wasn't!" At this point, I had to cut in to get us into a space for a private conversation.

RON: After moving into the meditation chapel, we continued. "So, from what I hear, it was you who administered your mother's medication under the hospital's direction. Correct?"

MARY: "Yes. And they told me she would go fast, but my mom was making all kinds of noises, and I kept calling and telling them I needed help and more medication, and they said they couldn't come because they were too busy. We all had to watch . . ."

RON: "If you don't mind my asking, how long was it from the time this started until she passed away?"

MARY: Still crying—there was no tissue in the chapel. "From about 7:00 a.m. until 6:00 in the evening, I had to watch her and they wouldn't help me!"

RON: "What took your mother?"

MARY: "Congestive heart failure."

RON: "You seem fearful. Are you reliving the experience here with your sister? This is a different situation in many respects."

MARY: "Yes. I remember what happened with Mother, and she kept grabbing and clutching my hand so hard. She struggled so much! The hospital wouldn't help me."

RON: "Mary, do you blame yourself for how this happened with your mother?"

MARY: As if a burden had been lifted, "Yes."

RON: "This is a difficult burden to carry, and it's so close to where you are with your sister. Have you told anyone about this up to now?"

MARY: "No. I know my mom's in heaven, but I have had no dreams about her since she died!" She starts to cry again.

RON: "It takes a lot of courage to share something like this. Thank you for doing that. I can't take away the feelings you have been carrying up to now in blaming yourself, but maybe I can help you work through it. As I've listened to your story, you were doing what the hospital was directing you to do because they couldn't be there. Is that how this went?"

MARY: "Yes. Each time I asked them to come they said they couldn't, and I needed to give her more medication." In Mary's mind, her mother was suffering greatly because of choking sounds the family endured.

RON: "So you acted the whole time on the directives of the hospital? That is, you were following their directions."

MARY: "Yes."

RON: "I do understand that you don't want to relive that trauma, but this is a different situation with your sister. It may or may not happen that way this time. Here she will be under the constant care of this hospital's medical staff. If she goes to comfort care status, she will be moved and be under constant watch. If you need a nurse or corpsman, they will be there."

MARY: With some relief, "That's good to hear."

RON: "You know, Mary, from where I'm sitting, I see a very caring daughter doing everything she could to assist her mother's final moments as best she could and following the direction she was given by the hospital. You did everything they said, right?"

MARY: "Yes, I did. But it was so long, and they said she would go quickly."

RON: "When it comes to cancer and ultimately heart failure, no one can predict how long patients will survive in those situations. You did all you could. Honestly, from all I have heard, I admire what you did. When my stepmom died of cancer in 2011, there were some similarities."

MARY: "I just don't want her to be mad at me. I know she's in heaven. She was a wonderful mother, but I hope she forgives me."

RON: "Being in heaven has a way of easing that kind of pain. But I have one idea, if you don't mind my sharing it with you. It may help."

MARY: "Yes, I'd like to hear it."

RON: "I don't share many of my stories in counseling unless I think it might be helpful to a situation. Years ago, when I was in a clinical pastoral residency—a training program for hospital chaplains—we had one resident among us who was really distant and not involved in the program. Not that he was unable to do the work, he was just unfeeling, and it led to some poor decisions on his part. I invested myself in helping him come along, as did the others in our unit. He was coming along for a while, and then suddenly he went back to his old ways. It came down to our supervisor having to end his participation in the program. I was very saddened by this, as I had put so much into helping him. One day, our supervisor told us we were going to remember him and his departure that day and directed us to write a letter to him. When all our letters were written, we gathered in a circle with one empty chair representing him and read our letters aloud. I can tell you I cried a lot when I read mine, and it was the most helpful thing for me. When we finished, she took us outside to the delivery area of the hospital and made us tear the letters apart. We were to never read them again. I can't tell you how healing it was."

MARY: She appears relieved. "I really like that idea."

RON: "I suggest taking as long as you want in writing your letter to your mother. Write until you feel it's complete. Then go to your mother's grave, by yourself. Bring a lawn chair, the letter, and some other gifts you may want to leave behind. After you get there, read the letter. It will be an emotional time. When you finish, completely destroy the letter. You will never need or want to read it again. This may be one way to help you with this."

MARY: "I like this. . . . I want to do this." She seems relieved. "Thank you so much for sharing this."

We spoke further, but this seemed to be the core issue of the conversation. I can say that, as far as I could see in further work with the family throughout the day, she was as ready as she could be for her sister's passing.

Evaluation

This was one of the more dynamic visits in recent memory. Many times, people hold back their greatest fears or unfinished business until they fall into times of crisis or loss such as this one. For months Mary was holding onto a burden of blame, and she came face-to-face with that burden when she began dealing with a new death situation. Her courage to go to this level in our discussion was admirable. Inside, I felt like I could only pray that the Lord would give me wisdom in dealing with this. It felt like I was treading on new ground. Why do I find ministry in the hospital the most meaningful? Visits like these—knowing you can help hurting people in such a time of need—makes this rewarding.

Feelings

On my end, I felt like much was accomplished by the conclusion of our visit. In spite of "feeling good"—and a little drained—after this visit, I knew that the "success" of this visit depended upon how Mary was doing as she continued working through the process of seeing her sister in this ongoing stage of dying. As I further ministered to Mary and the family, and as I observed her speech and body language, she appeared relieved after that visit. She was not only at peace but walked her dad through the process as well. In addition, as I sat in on the family meeting with the doctors, the family was relieved as they were assured that assistance was available to make certain her sister would have a peaceful passing.

Reflection

In thinking about this visit and the burden of guilt and blame that Mary carried, I couldn't help but think about David and the burden he had carried after his sin with Bathsheba. Not that I believe Mary committed sin; she did all she could to ease her mother's journey. It was what she laid on herself that became the burden. Yes, David made a horrible choice that caused him to carry a shameful burden as well, but Psalm 32:3–4 describes so well what seemed to be Mary's burden. It reads:

> When I kept silent,
>> my bones wasted away
>> through my groaning all day long.
> For day and night
>> your hand was heavy on me;
> my strength was sapped
>> as in the heat of summer.

There is the burden of sin, no doubt, but there is also the burden of what we place upon ourselves. I think that's what was happening with Mary. In the end, I felt privileged and humbled to play a part in helping relieve the burden she had been carrying for months.

Future Response

At this point, there is no future response. The patient passed at the beginning of March. However, I would be happy to provide further assistance to the sister or the family if they contact me at the hospital. I have invited them to do so. Up to this point, I have not received any contact from the family. This family had their own church and minister, so I assume they moved in that direction after she passed.

HYBRID APPROACH

Another way to approach creating a ministry artifact is to use multiple verbatim episodes that revolve around the same issue. Below is an example of a minister who drew from the strengths of a case study approach and the verbatim form.

A Leadership Challenge
Background Information

This interaction involves Pastor Smith (not his real name) and me (John). Pastor Smith is the senior pastor of City Church (CC), and I am the associate pastor. We have seven full-time staff, and church attendance runs approximately 600 adults on Sunday mornings. Including children, we have approximately 1100 that claim City Church as their home.

Pastor Smith has been the senior pastor for over twenty-five years. He is in his mid-60s. He planted a church that merged with CC and then became the pastor of the new (blended) congregation. About ten years ago, I merged the church I was pastoring with CC and became the associate pastor. I planned to move on to another pastorate quickly. But doors never opened, so I remained. In the hope of opening more doors, I chose to begin my doctorate. Pastor Smith had written a glowing reference to help me get into a nearby seminary and had asked about the program a few times.

This interaction relates to the pursuit of my doctorate while I was a staff member.

> **JOHN:** "Hey, pastor. I was wondering if we could talk for a few minutes."
>
> **PASTOR SMITH:** "Sure, come on in."
>
> **JOHN:** "You know I am looking ahead to my doctoral program, and the program seminars run for three weeks a year—two in the summer and one in the winter. It's the same schedule as Pastor Tim." Tim is an assistant pastor who is also starting his doctorate through another seminary. "I am committed to this process for my personal growth, and it has a benefit for the church, so I was hoping you might consider allowing me to count all, or at least

some, of this training as work time rather than vacation time. As it stands right now, I get three weeks of vacation, and that means for the next three years I would have no time away with my family, but I would be away from my family for an extended period to progress in my studies." I attempted to keep this serious but humble. I wanted to give some reasons, including benefit to the church and the importance of family, to motivate what I knew was generally going to be an uphill struggle.

PASTOR SMITH: "We don't do that here, so it will count as vacation time if you want to do it."

JOHN: "I know we don't have a policy, so it's really an issue of philosophy at this point. That is why I was hoping you might consider it."

PASTOR SMITH: "No, it's not going to happen."

JOHN: "I would ask you to think about it and pray about it, and I will check in with you in a few days. I hope you will be willing to consider it." At this point I changed the direction of our conversation to other issues and then returned a few days later.

JOHN: "Hey, pastor, I was wondering if you had a chance to think any more about the request I made about my doctoral program."

PASTOR SMITH: "Yes, I thought about it, and the answer is still no."

JOHN: "I think this is important and worthy of discussion. Would you be willing to talk with the elders about a potential policy for continuing education?" There was a long pause that made me anxious. I knew I was going over his head by not taking his word as the final answer, but his view of education and support of his staff has never been affirming. Though technically he is considered an equal on the elder board, he holds significant sway due to his tenure and chairmanship of the board. After what seemed like an eternity, he answered.

PASTOR SMITH: "I will bring it to the elders, but I will speak firmly against it." His response did surprise me, as it seemed driven by being offended by my failure to yield to his first no. I don't know that he was angry, but it was clear that he was going to ensure the answer remained no.

JOHN: "Thanks for being willing to get their input."

PASTOR SMITH: "We have a meeting in two weeks; remind me before the meeting."

I decided to write a letter to the elders to explain the doctoral program, its benefit, and to humbly request consideration for all or half the time of the program to count as work time. I chose not to deal with the finances of the program, just my request about my continuing education counting in some sense as work time.

JOHN: "Hey, pastor, I decided to write a note to the elders to explain some things about the doctoral program. If you are willing, I would like either to send it to them, or you can give it to them. Let me know if that is okay with you."

PASTOR SMITH: "I will attach it to the packet I give the elders at the meeting."

I sent the letter to Pastor Smith by email.

A week later the meeting happened. Only one of our associate staff is on the elder board, but he was able to give me an understanding of what took place in the elders meeting. Essentially, Pastor Smith invited the elders to read the letter without comment. He asked if anyone wanted to open the issue for discussion (someone did). He then told them he wanted them to discuss it before he gave his input. The group discussed, asked questions, evaluated the need and benefit of the program, considered the staff who would be immediately impacted, and wondered if other staff might be interested in the creation of a policy. Overall, according to the staff member, it was positive and seemed to be moving in a direction that would have benefited the staff and their educational pursuits. After the discussion among the elders ended, Pastor Smith said, "I told Pastor John I would speak against this," and then he did. He did not see value in the doctoral program because it was not necessary for me to do my assigned tasks. The church did not ask us to enter the program; therefore, the church was not responsible for it. It would be like giving special staff three extra weeks of vacation. In the end, the vote was three to two against the creation of a policy.

Reflection

1. **Evaluation**
   a. **What happened?** I asked the elders to consider creating a policy for the staff to participate in extended learning opportunities.
   b. **Why did it happen?** I am an advocate by nature and practice, and I felt it was important to bring this need for both myself and the other staff who want to continue their education.
   c. **What was your role?** Staff advocate, instigator.
   d. **What would have happened if you did not push past the original no?** Nothing would have happened. I don't think there was another way to be heard.
   e. **What were the turning points?** When I asked Pastor Smith if he was willing to take it to the elders.
   f. **What are your hunches?** I knew he was going to say no, so I had preplanned to ask him to seek the elders' counsel on the matter. I know he is not an advocate for his staff or himself, so I knew it was unlikely that he would say yes. At that same time, he would not say no to the request for review by the elders. What I didn't expect was for him to speak against it.

2. **Feelings**
   a. **About the people in the incident:** Disappointed that Pastor Smith could have been an advocate but instead spoke against it. Disappointed that the elders used their perception of our gifting and the need for the training based solely on its benefit to CC.
   b. **About the incident:** Unsupported, discouraged, and unvalued as a pastor who has served faithfully for ten years.
   c. **About yourself:** I feel angry. Maybe bitter at times.
   d. **How did they change during the incident?** My loss of motivation.

3. **Theological Reflection**
   a. **What were the theological assumptions (conscious and unconscious) of persons involved (including you)? Was there consistency between assumptions and actions?** Pastor Smith received an MA in Bible and did that because he felt he needed to rather than because it was beneficial for ministry.

Due to the school he chose and his experience, he basically writes off that experience as not beneficial and questions the need for anything above an MDiv at this point. He feels we have been given specific roles at the church, and we don't need more education to fulfill our given role. He uses superficial and philosophical views to evaluate the gifts of others and determines their usefulness rather than lifting them up and helping them fulfill the role they desire.[5]

b. **What theology was at work during the incident?** Authority, eldership, humility, pride.

c. **How did these theological issues relate to Christian biblical and historical tradition?** Eldership and pastoral roles that are defined by historical traditions.

4. **Future response**

   a. **By the evaluation you have given, what needs to be done now?** At present, there is nothing to be done about this policy issue. If given the opportunity, I will continue to express my disagreement on this issue and continue to be an advocate for our staff.

   b. **What will you do next to minister in the situation?** I will continue to fulfill my role and hope for changes in the future.

PROCESSING CASE STUDIES AND VERBATIM REPORTS

While the author of the case study or verbatim report engages in some theological reflection, the mentor or peer group that processes the events with the person involved in the ministry can add depth and breadth of understanding to the events.

Whether being processed with a mentor or in a peer group, there are several key commitments.

---

5. Notice that the author of this artifact did not analyze his own theological assumptions. It is often the case that those new to the experience are not comfortable fully exposing their assumptions. It has been my (Wilson) practice not to force students to self-disclose beyond their comfort zone for class assignments.

1. Everyone involved commits to the confidential nature of the case study or verbatim report.[6] Real names are never used.
2. The people depicted in a case study or verbatim report are real people, and many times the stories include both the fragile and resilient nature of life itself.
3. The sharing of each verbatim should begin with a prayer asking for God's counsel and close with a prayer lifting up the individuals represented in the verbatim.

Processing with a Mentor

When processing a verbatim with a mentor, the experience will be one-on-one, which allows for a more direct and intimate level of discussion. Based on the trust and depth of the relationship, this engagement has the potential to move directly to the kind of processing needed most by the presenter. The real value in a one-on-one mentor relationship hinges on the attitude and position of the mentor. A Japanese proverb says, "If he works for you, you work for him." The passion and effort the mentor puts into the life of a mentee carries extraordinary influence and weight in the mentoring relationship.

Advantages of processing with an individual mentor include:

- One-on-one, individualized attention
- Opportunity to focus on the specific needs of the mentee
- Building depth into the relationship for ongoing future support

Individual mentors must understand the basic leadership principles of their role and understand supervision or mentoring as a ministry to the person they are leading. These principles include:

---

6. We should never underestimate the importance of the rule of confidentiality when it comes to working through a case study or verbatim. In a ministry practicum class in San Quentin State Prison, a class of eight inmates was working through a verbatim. The presentation went as planned with open, honest, and rich discussion. The next week prior to class, the student presenter from the previous week approached the professor and indicated there was a problem. He reported that someone in the group had gone to the individual from the verbatim and told him the group had discussed him in great detail. The person who was the focal point of the verbatim confronted the presenting student and threatened him. In class, the professor dealt with the confidential nature of working with people in ministry. The evening was engaging to say the least. By the end of class, the person who had broken confidentiality agreed to go back to the upset inmate who had been the subject of discussion and calm the water. The student inmate who presented the verbatim did not have to fight, and everyone learned a valuable lesson about confidentiality.

- All persons are of value.
- Leaders must be servants.
- Leaders must equip others.
- Leaders must empower others.
- Leaders must encourage others.
- Leaders must enrich others spiritually.
- Leaders must enhance the kingdom of God.
- Leaders must be accountable.

Processing with a Peer Group

Processing a ministry artifact with a peer group should occur only with others who are actively engaged in ministry. With the understanding that each member of the group will have an opportunity to serve as the presenter to the group, the Golden Rule immediately kicks in and the trust level begins to deepen. An ideal group size would be at least six to ten people including the presenter. Groups too small will lose the dynamic of idea exchange as the group members interact. If the group is too large, the conversation becomes crowded, and some will choose not to participate. The actual size of the group may vary within these limits, but as the group grows in their relationship to one another, the freedom of conversation will also grow.

Once presenters have shared their ministry artifact, and the group has the opportunity to read it carefully, a group facilitator should invite the group to ask clarifying questions. It is important for each member of the group to have a clear understanding of the people represented in the ministry artifact and the ways they contribute, as well as the dynamics at work in the situation. After the clarifying questions, the presenter articulates what they hope to discover in the ensuing conversation.

At this point, presenters observe silently and take notes, as the group unpacks the ministry artifact using the reflection loop. The group will begin by listing the various issues that surfaced during the reading and subsequent clarifying question time. Some issues will be apparent, and some will be lodged in the hidden areas not articulated. Group members will learn to read between the lines and discover issues not stated or even visible in the mind of the presenter at the time of writing the ministry artifact.

The group should not attempt to resolve the issues that surface but instead should focus on creating clarity in looking back on the ministry experience. As the group looks back from different vantage points, listeners with various viewpoints might discover elements the presenters did not. By having the presenters observe silently, they can focus on listening—an overlooked skill in ministry engagement. Too often, we are quick to speak, and we fail to listen, even though Scripture reminds us to "be quick to listen, slow to speak and slow to become angry" (James 1:19).

After a time of identifying and aligning the issues and discussing their potential impact, the group moves to interpreting the incident in order to explore the possibilities. Remind the group the task is not to fix anything but to gain a clearer understanding of the dynamics of the situation.

Exploring involves understanding why circumstances have moved in the direction they have and includes discussing possible actions that might apply a positive influence on the story. These are simply ideas spelled out for consideration after a time of careful deliberation on the issues involved. Before discussion wanes, the facilitator calls this portion of the session to a close and invites the presenter back into the conversation.

The presenters of the ministry artifact get the last word. They summarize what they heard. Often, there is an attitude of thanksgiving to the group for providing a magnitude of new considerations and things over which to ponder and pray.

By the end of the session, it is time to pray. What began with a general prayer for the Lord to guide the direction of the meeting will end with specific prayers for the circumstance, each person involved, and for the presenters as they leave this safe environment and move back into their respective worlds of ministry, influencing the lives of real people.

Advantages of peer group processing include:

- Presenters have an opportunity to clarify how and what they wrote in the verbatim.
- The questions can teach them how to write such a document in the future.
- The presenter can listen intently as their peers sift through the details like crime scene investigators. Ideas not yet given serious attention can come into focus.

- Finally, the presenter has an opportunity to summarize to the group what they have heard. This is accomplished within the confines of the safe setting of their peer group.

The Golden Rule allows them to honor the thoughts and considerations of their peers, as they will later have opportunity to speak similar words of wisdom to their colleagues. The depth of conversation and insight is limited to the level of trust the group has created together. Therefore, a newly formed group cannot go into the same depth as a group that has been together and bonded over time and through experience.

CHAPTER 8

PLANNING FOR PROFESSIONAL AND PERSONAL GROWTH

> ### At a Glance
>
> - A growth covenant has historical roots and theological significance.
> - A growth covenant works toward the successful completion of goals and does not focus on penalties for nonperformance.

Have you ever asked God to search you and test you? Have you prayed David's prayer, "Search me, God, and know my heart; test me and know my anxious thoughts. See if there is any offensive way in me, and lead me in the way everlasting" (Ps. 139:23–24)? To some degree, theological reflection is a means of praying that prayer. When operating with honesty and integrity, those who practice theological reflection are seeking to please God more and be more effective as ministers of the gospel. The growth covenant is a crucial tool to help you do that.

Sometimes the gaps you identify between your operational and confessed theology, theory, or emotional health can be covered by on-the-spot adjustments. Other gaps that surface during the reflection loop require a more intentional and rigorous process to close. With a concerted effort, you can experience incremental change over a period of a few months. Even so, some needs could require a lifetime of attention.

COVENANTING: CLARIFYING YOUR INTENTIONS FOR GROWTH

A growth covenant is a theological reflection tool that allows ministers to plan for the *closing of the gap* through an intentional growth plan. It is not a legal contract protecting against nonperformance. It is a covenant formalizing an agreement to promote promise keeping.

God created multiple covenants with Old Testament Israel and New Testament believers.[1]

The Old Testament idea of covenant emerges from this legal understanding, with the root Hebrew idea being "to bind," or a "bond" between two parties.[2] But the unique biblical understanding of covenant is found in the unbalanced covenants between God and his people. Whereas a covenant between humans is between equal parties, such an agreement between God and humans is one-sided. "The contracting parties stood on entirely different levels. The covenant constituted an announcement of God's will to extend gracious benefits to those willing to receive them, binding themselves to him by ties of absolute obligation."[3] Motivated by lovingkindness, God pledged to the Israelites, "You will be my people, and I will be your God" (Jer. 11:4; Ezek. 11:20; Zech. 8:8). Furthermore, an Old Testament covenant was typically seen as a permanently binding agreement (Deut. 7:9).[4]

The New Testament (new covenant) emphasizes the same unbalanced nature (Rom. 5:6–8). Given God's initiative and grace through Jesus's sacrificial action, the new covenant is also "an arrangement made by one party with plenary power [i.e., God] that the other party [i.e., humans] may accept or reject but cannot alter."[5]

The theme of covenant runs throughout Scripture, but its theological significance includes what God did with an already recognized legal concept. A covenant is essentially a contract, an agreement between two

---

1. The word "testament" is another word for covenant.
2. Gleason L. Archer Jr., "Covenant," *Evangelical Dictionary of Theology*, ed. Daniel J. Treier, 3rd ed. (Grand Rapids: Baker Academic, 2017), 214.
3. Archer, "Covenant," 214.
4. However, the question remains as to the conditional or unconditional nature of the Old Testament covenant, based on Israel's obedience or lack thereof. Answering this question is beyond the scope of this discussion.
5. Archer, "Covenant," 215.

parties "binding them mutually to undertakings on each other's behalf."[6] Covenants at their core are more relational than contractual. The strength of the relationship motivates both parties to work together to accomplish the terms of the covenant.

Covenants are formed between one party (covenantor) who promises the other party (covenantee) to do something (affirmative covenant) or not do something (negative covenant) according to the terms of the agreement. While a covenant is a type of contract, there is a subtle difference between the two. Contracts are set up to discourage failure. Detailed contractual obligations and nonperformance penalties keep both parties honest. But a covenant focuses on the promise at the heart of the agreement. Signatories to the covenant are motivated to fulfill the agreement by the uncoerced promise they made, not by whether they can avoid defaulting.

The theological reflection tool known as the growth covenant builds on the legal and biblical understandings of covenant. While the growth covenant is not a legally binding agreement, its value is enhanced if all parties approach the agreement with the same gravity as a legal agreement. The minister will gain the most from this agreement if it is approached with the level of commitment that God approached people in his promises: permanent and unwavering commitment motivated by dedicated lovingkindness (and fulfillment, regardless of the other's lack of commitment).

—————————————— *Reflections* ——————————————

"Developing a covenant was a very helpful and meaningful exercise for me. Its structure and purpose caused me to examine the motives and desired outcomes for my life and ministry. One of my goals translated into a detailed discipleship pathway, which has given birth to second- and third-generation disciple makers. This was a direct result of this initiative. This was not an academic exercise for me. It resulted in real ministry outcomes with long-term kingdom ramifications."

6. Archer, "Covenant," 214.

SETTING COVENANT GOALS

What Are My Growth Needs?

Using the reflection loop, you have learned the need to align your operational theology with your confessed theology. After identifying the operational theology (what your actions communicate that you believe or think or feel) and comparing that with your confessed theology (what you say you believe), you notice a gap between the two. The next step is to work at closing that gap so your actions will better reflect your understanding of God's truth.

Reflections

"Through my growth covenant, I was able to identify areas where my professed theology differed from my life and ministry practice. I knew that many of my actions demonstrated a misalignment with what I said I believed. Once I began reflecting and journaling, I was horrified to discover how substantial the misalignments were. It was amazing how quickly the Lord initiated the alignment process. It appears that he was waiting for me to realize these sins, to repent of them, and then do the required alignment. He graciously collaborated with me to initiate healing and start me on a trajectory toward integrity."

In describing a growth need, do not build a presumed solution or action into the need statement. For instance, if your car has a tire that is losing air, you would tell the tire-store attendant, "My front driver's-side tire is losing air." You wouldn't say, "Would you please add some air to my front driver's-side tire?" Adding air might solve the problem for a few days, but it will not bring about a more permanent solution if the tire has a hole. If you ask the attendant to add air, likely that is what she will do. But if there is a bad valve stem or a slow leak, adding air will not solve the problem. Your tire will continue to leak air.

In conversation, we often say things like, "I need an aspirin," instead of saying, "My head hurts—I have a headache." Building the solution into the need statement keeps you from finding the root cause. For instance, at a high altitude the headache may be signaling dehydration, and in that case aspirin will actually work against the solution.[7]

The key to writing a clear need statement is to write about the identified gap—why is your current condition less than the ideal you are striving for? After you have described the gap, you can envision what could and should be in your life—a new end state.

What Is the Desired End State (Goal)?

While our desired end state could go all the way into eternity, the goal statement will look forward to a specific point in time when you wish to achieve an incremental improvement over your current condition. The goal states what needs to change in you personally.

For example, if you wrote, "My Body Mass Index (BMI) of 27 is outside of the recommended healthy range for a person my age." Then your goal might be "I will reduce my BMI from 27 to 24.9 over the next twelve months." If accomplished, the goal BMI would put the person in the healthy range.

However, if the BMI was 32, the goal might be "I will reduce my BMI from 32 to below 30 over the next twelve months." The goal of "below 30" is still not in the healthy range, but it is outside of the "obese" designation and would be a legitimate twelve-month goal.

A good goal includes three things:

1. A clear description of what could and should be (reduced BMI)
2. Measurable markers (from 27 to 24.9)
3. A fixed timeline (twelve months)

The goal statement directly relates to the need statement. It provides an "after picture" to the need statement's "before picture." The goal statement does not contain methodology. It does not mention what action steps you plan on taking to bring about the desired change. That comes in the next section of the growth covenant.

---

7. E. Turlejska and M. A. Baker, "Aspirin Enhances Evaporation in Hydrated and Dehydrated Rats," *Canadian Journal of Physiology and Pharmacology* 66, no. 1 (January 1988): 72–76, https://www.ncbi.nlm.nih.gov/pubmed/3370538.

Reflections

"One of my covenant goals was to improve my devotional life. Spending more time with God has opened more of my life to him so he has more control. Because I spend more time praying, and my prayers have become more intentional, my experience with God has improved. This has helped me listen to God and refrain from thinking I know what's best for my life.

"This is a huge change for me. I learned that God wants to help me and that he does when I get out of the way. My new devotional life affirmed that God would help me and improve my life if I let go and make room for him to be the Lord of my life. This has encouraged me and shown that I am on the right path in my walk of faith. My life has become a richer testimony for Jesus.

"My family, church members, and others have recognized the difference. They wonder why I am so happy and content. They show their appreciation for how I listen to them more attentively. I can tell them it is because my relationship with God is greater and improves every day."

What Action Steps Will I Take?

Before GPS apps can map a route, they first must determine where you are currently. You must provide your desired location and indicate what means you want to use to get to your destination: automobile, mass transit, or walking.

In this analogy, your *need statement* corresponds to where you are, your *goal statement* corresponds to where you want to be, and your *action step(s)* corresponds to the means of transportation. The action steps are what you are going to do to accomplish your goal. For example:

Need: My BMI of 27 is outside of the recommended healthy range for a person my age.

Goal: I will reduce my BMI from 27 to 24.9 over the next twelve months.

Action Steps:

1. I will use the "Lose It" app on my smartphone to record my calorie intake every day for a year.

2. I will take at least 10,000 steps for five of seven days of each week and will total around 70,000 per week for forty-five of fifty-two weeks.

3. On days I exceed my recommended caloric intake, I will note in my ministry journal what food choices I made that resulted in overeating. I will also note in what context the choice was made, such as:

   a. Did I overeat as self-medication for stress?

   b. Did I overeat due to social pressure?

   c. Was I in a situation where my choices were limited?

4. I will locate and read a credible book on healthy eating.

Each action step contributes to reaching the goal. Notice that some of the action steps integrate another theological reflection tool. This example references the ministry journal and how it can be used on days when the person overeats. By entering that data in the journal, the minister can include a search for overeating patterns. If a pattern emerges, such as overeating in social settings when food choices are limited, then the minister can choose to eat a small nutritious meal before the social setting to curb the inclination to overeat at the event. Without recording the data, the insight would be missed.

The theological reflection tools also interact as they aid in selecting the needs to be addressed in the growth covenant. For instance, if a ministry journal evaluation reveals that a minister tends to grow frustrated and become reactive during conflict situations, it might indicate a need for growth in ministering amid conflict. Or while a mentor is processing a verbatim (chap. 7) with the minister, he or she might identify the minister's tendency to pull rank on subordinates during disagreements. This might spark a growth covenant goal about becoming more collegial with staff members.

After the action steps are enumerated, the only thing left to do is to determine the evaluative criteria for whether or not the goal was accomplished.

How Will I Evaluate the Goal?

In the case of our BMI reduction example, the ultimate evaluation of the goal is the new measurement. But that is not the only way the goal should be evaluated. There should be both output (Was the new BMI achieved?) and input (Did I follow the plan?) evaluations. Notice that even the action steps are written in measurable terms.

Need: My BMI of 27 is outside of the recommended healthy range for a person my age.

Goal: I will reduce my BMI from 27 to 24.9 over the next twelve months.

Action Steps:

1. I will use the "Lose It" app on my smartphone to record my calorie intake every day for a year.
2. I will take at least 10,000 steps for five of seven days of each week and will total around 70,000 per week for forty-five of fifty-two weeks.
3. On days I exceed my recommended caloric intake, I will note in my ministry journal what food choices I made that resulted in overeating. I will also note in what context the choice was made, such as:
    a. Did I overeat as self-medication for stress?
    b. Did I overeat due to social pressure?
    c. Was I in a situation where my choices were limited?
4. I will locate and read a credible book on healthy eating.

Measurements:

1. After entering my measurements in a BMI Calculator,[8] did I reduce my BMI from 27 to 24.9 after twelve months?
2. Did I enter my entire food intake in the "Lose It" app every day for a year?
3. Did I reach my step goal at least forty-five weeks of the year?
4. Did I reach a conclusion about why I commonly overeat?
5. Did I locate and read a book on good nutrition?

---

8. For instance, see https://www.nhlbi.nih.gov/health/educational/lose_wt/BMI/bmicalc .htm

In this example, the first evaluative criterion is an *output* measurement: Did I reach the goal? The others are *input* measurements: Did I follow the plan? Both are important, especially if I did not reach the output goal. If I failed to reach the output goal, but I did follow the plan, I learn that I need to get a new plan. If I didn't follow the plan, then I need to do some soul searching about why I failed to follow through.

As you develop your growth covenant, you want to address both professional and personal growth needs. Those within your 360° support system might be able to identify areas where you could grow. You may also discover needs on your own as you write verbatims, case studies, and ministry journal entries. Luke 2:52 establishes another source for ideas. After telling how twelve-year-old Jesus visited the temple, Luke comments on the growth Jesus experienced in the intervening years: "Jesus grew in wisdom and stature, and in favor with God and man" (Luke 2:52). He grew intellectually, physically, spiritually, and relationally. These categories are helpful for developing your covenant goals.[9]

Growth Covenant Sample

The following growth covenant sample is for a student intern working in a ministry field selected for the purpose of their theological field education course. The covenant preamble contains details negotiated between the intern and supervisor that clarify expectations. Educational institutions would likely not require doctoral candidates to include a preamble in their covenant.

Covenant Preamble

Student Intern: Johnny Intern
Degree Program: MDiv, third-year student
Vocational goal: Pastor
Covenant Dates: August 29 to May 19

9. Ed Rowell, *Go the Distance: 21 Habits & Attitudes for Winning at Life* (Nashville: B&H, 2002), 166.

Field Mentor:

Pastor Under Shepherd

Community Church in Any Town, USA, for the last five years

Thirty-three years total pastoral experience

Graduate of Exceptional Seminary

Ministry Setting:

Community Church

1234 Somewhere Street

Any Town, USA

Telephone: (909) 555-0123

Setting Description: Community Church is forty-five years old with an average worship attendance of 125 and 200 total members. The church has eighteen middle and high school students to be engaged in ministry. The church is located forty miles from the seminary campus.

Ministry Position: Youth Minister/Young Adult Bible Study Teacher. Responsibilities include leading and teaching weekly youth group meetings, coordinating all special events related to middle school and high school students, serving on the teaching team for a young adult home study group, and preaching in the Sunday service on an "as-needed" basis.

Weekly Time Expectations:

Sunday evening:	2
Mentor meeting:	1
Worship service:	1
Weekly home group:	2
Elder meeting:	2
Preparation Time:	2
Total estimated ministry hours:	10

Other Expectations:
- Become a member of Community Church and participate in all church-related activities.
- Subject to membership and employment policies.
- Participate in weekly elder meetings.
- Preach to the congregation at the discretion and request of the pastor.

Covenant Body

Ministry Goal 1

Need: I often feel awkward when relating to teenagers and am not confident in my overall ability to relate well with middle and high school students.

Goal: Initiate, develop, and nurture youth ministry skills by May 19, which will allow me to guide students on their disciple journey toward maturity in Christ.

Actions:
1. Research the *National Study of Youth & Religion* website (youthandreligion.nd.edu).
2. Read *Teenagers Matter* by Mark Cannister.
3. Journal three key takeaways from reading *Teenagers Matter* and discuss with mentors.
4. Establish an outside network of two to three youth ministry leaders for ongoing learning and fellowship and meet with them quarterly.
5. Provide direction for the Sunday morning Bible study leaders.
6. Meet weekly as a youth group on Sunday nights for fellowship and discipleship.
7. Prepare weekly messages and training for the Sunday night sessions.
8. Develop and plan outside youth events for student outreach and fellowship.

9. Discuss learning, messages, and plans with my field mentor for guidance.

Evaluation:

1. Meet weekly with my field mentor and monthly with my spiritual mentor to discuss progress in gaining appropriate youth ministry skills.

2. Evaluate progress in December and May with mentors to assess my growth in the ministry.

3. Request periodic feedback from the students and parents on progress of the youth ministry from August to May.

Ministry Goal 2

Need: While I have experience preaching in multigenerational environments, I have never preached to a congregation composed mostly of students.

Goal: Develop preaching and teaching skills to effectively communicate God's Word to our students by May.

Actions:

1. Review seminary class texts and notes from my preaching, hermeneutics, and "Principles and Approaches to Bible Teaching" courses.

2. Carefully study the passages that I will preach or teach from.

3. Read *Text-Driven Preaching* by Akin, Allen, and Mathews to deepen my understanding of preaching.

4. Journal three key takeaways from reading *Text-Driven Preaching* and discuss with mentors.

5. Receive input from my field mentor for preparing messages to preach and teach.

6. Record sessions when preaching or teaching for evaluation.

Evaluation:

1. Listen to and evaluate recordings of my teaching and preaching.

2. Request peer evaluation from other seminary students at the church.
3. Receive feedback on recordings from my mentors.
4. Listen to critique from my wife without getting defensive.
5. Evaluate progress in December and May with mentors to assess my growth.
6. Ask student representatives of the youth council to provide feedback on my communication skills.

Personal Goal

Need: I often get defensive in conflict situations. People sometimes find me unapproachable after a confrontation.

Goal: By the end of the class, I will assess with my mentors the improvement of my direct style of communication and overall presence when confronting.

Actions:

1. Read *The Peacemaker* by Ken Sande to learn how to resolve conflict.
2. Journal three key takeaways from reading *The Peacemaker* and discuss with mentors.
3. Review notes and readings from pastoral ministry classes to be reminded on how to conduct myself around people.
4. Pray and read my Bible to understand the grace I have received in order to understand how to give grace to others.
5. Ask mentors to assist me in being a better listener and to ask more questions.
6. Practice clarifying comments or questions before jumping to conclusions.
7. Journal times of confrontational interaction with people.

Evaluation:

1. Discuss and evaluate progress with my mentors at our scheduled meetings.

2. Discuss and evaluate with my wife after interacting with people at church.
3. Review the tracked growth from my journal regarding my approach and overall presence with my mentors in December and May.

Spiritual Growth

Need: I am not consistent in practicing spiritual disciplines.

Goal: I will develop a structure that promotes faithfulness for me in following a spiritual growth plan.

Actions:

1. Engage in a daily Bible reading plan from August to May.
2. Create a prayer list of concerns to focus on daily from August to May.
3. Add weekly updates to the prayer list.
4. Reflect theologically on how God intersects with my life.
5. Make at least three journal entries per week until December.
6. Make at least five journal entries per week from January to May.
7. Identify in my journal time-wasters in my life that can be eliminated.

Evaluation:

1. Personal evaluation: Did I stay consistent with the plan?
2. Periodically review my journal with my mentors.
3. What identifiable benefits do I recognize in myself?
4. What did I learn about God and his desires for my life and ministry?
5. Mentor evaluation: What do they see in me after nine months in the program?
6. What will I do differently going forward after the program?

Evangelism Goal

Need: While I understand the gospel and accept my responsibility to be active in the Great Commission within my sphere of influence, I do not practice sharing my faith on a regular basis. I have noticed that the students I serve do not either.

Goal: I will be more regular and systematic in sharing the gospel with people in our community and will encourage our students to do the same.

Actions:

1. Teach the gospel to youth from August to December.
2. Train every student to write and articulate his or her testimony by December.
3. Demonstrate and practice simulated gospel presentations from August to December.
4. Discuss how to look for opportunities to present from August to December.
5. Go into the community to have gospel-centric conversations with people from December to May.
6. Encourage every student to invite at least one person from these encounters to one of our youth events.

Evaluation:

1. Evaluate each student's ability to communicate the gospel and his or her testimony clearly.
2. How many students have increased their comfort level in sharing the gospel?
3. How many gospel conversations did I have?
4. How many people came to the church because of our efforts?
5. How many people made a decision to follow Jesus during the program?

Covenant Signatures

We have read and are in agreement with this ministry practicum covenant that consists of the ministry description, time commitment, and goals related to ministry, personhood, spiritual, and evangelism areas of the student's life. We enter into this covenant relationship to carry out our agreements for the duration of this internship. We understand that this covenant may be adjusted periodically and renegotiated as needed.

Minister: _____

Mentor: _____

WORKING WITH YOUR GROWTH COVENANT

If you are a student, your educational institution might require other parties to be signatories to your covenant. Otherwise, the covenant will at minimum require your signature and your mentor's signature. While the growth covenant is primarily between you and God, your mentor will help you develop it, make mid-course adjustments as you are following the covenant, and provide you with accountability.

Developing the Covenant

You will spend a good bit of time developing your growth covenant during mentoring sessions. Your mentor will provide guidance to keep you from being overly aggressive and unrealistic and to caution you if you are not diagnosing the gap between your theology and practice accurately. Mentees are often too hard on themselves, and there are occasionally ministers who don't lean into disciplines like this sufficiently. Your mentor can be asked to guide you through the developmental stage, which will range from several weeks to several months.

Implementing the Covenant

As you are following your covenant, there will be times that you will get discouraged and will need your mentor to come alongside you and cheer you on. Other times, you will need some accountability to do what you intended to do. It is easy to let life events swallow up your good intentions. Ultimately, this is your plan. It is what you have determined will help you grow as a minister and a person, and it is up to you to follow the plan.

Evaluating the Covenant

You will do some evaluation on your own, but much of it will be done in mentoring sessions as you look at what you accomplished and what goals you did not reach. Your mentor will help you celebrate God's grace in your life and explore what changes you can make in your plan to attempt to close the gap between your need statement and goal statement.

While it is possible to make real-time evaluations about whether or not mentees are successful at accomplishing a covenant goal, it is more difficult to determine if ministers achieve ministry success. Just as it is possible to win a battle and lose a war, some ministers accomplish their goals but never reach their full potential. Some would point to numerical success or expanded influence as the ultimate indicator of success, but it is possible to enjoy all of the appearances of success and not finish well in ministry, casting a negative shadow on a life of service.

We hope every minister will keep the long view in mind while setting incremental growth goals in the covenant, which will be easier to do after considering what constitutes ministry success.

CHAPTER 9

MINISTERIAL SUCCESS

At a Glance

- While theological reflection is done "in the middle of things," it happens with an awareness of the endings that follow.
- Ministers' views of success must take into account the call to be obedient and faithful.
- Measuring success must also include tangible results.

Implicit in viewing theological reflection as occurring "in the middle of things" (chap. 2) is the realization that things happen before and after it. In chapter 6, we explored one of the issues ministers face in the beginning of things, namely, their call to ministry leadership. It is fitting to remember the beginning while in the middle of things. The beginning—that is, our call to ministry leadership—reminds us why we are doing what we are doing and why we want to do it well. Because of our desire to fulfill our calling, we use the reflection loop (chap. 3) to identify, align, and explore ways to be more faithful and effective in fulfilling our calling.

But it is also helpful to remember the end while "in the middle of things." We want to say with the apostle Paul, "I have fought the good fight, I have finished the race, I have kept the faith" (2 Tim. 4:7). So as we come to the end of this conversation about theological reflection, we pause for a moment to consider what it means to finish well. What is success in ministry?

Some aspects of ministry success are quantifiable by numbers—the size of the church, amount of the compensation package, or growth percentage.

Other signs of success are less objective. Real success has more to do with *obedience*, *faithfulness*, and achieving one's *potential* than the size of a church or retirement fund. Reaching goals and having influence are certainly important, but if you do those things and lose your integrity along the way, it is hard to consider yourself a success.

OBEDIENCE

"The whole of biblical theology," Gary Burge argues, "centers on divine revelation and receptive human response: God speaks his word; we hear and must obey."[1] Obeying God is at the very heart of understanding him, living in the fullness of the eternal life he provides, and, certainly, ministering in his name.

Obedience Is Assumed after a Person Hears

The Hebrew and Greek words of the Old and New Testaments convey the double meaning of hearing and obeying. The assumption is that when God's people heard him speak, they would instantly obey. Charles Stanley says, "When the Holy Spirit speaks to an obedient person's heart, that person doesn't even stop to consider whether he will act. He responds instantly."[2]

In the Old Testament, God's law demanded responsive obedience (Ex. 19:5); hearing God's rules necessitated the responsibility of obedience. Abraham exemplified this level of hearing-obedience (Gen. 22:18). The prophets railed against Israel for supposedly hearing but not obeying God (Jer. 3:13). They have "ears to hear but do not hear, for they are a rebellious house" (Ezek. 12:2).[3]

Jesus amplified this idea when he said, "Whoever has ears, let them hear" (Matt. 11:15; Mark 4:9; Luke 14:35). Such commands from the Master demand immediate response: now that you have heard, do something! Jesus called people to excellent character expressed through right attitudes *and* right actions.

---

1. G. M. Burge, "Obedience," *Evangelical Dictionary of Theology*, ed. Daniel J. Treier, 3rd ed. (Grand Rapids: Baker Academic, 2017), 606.
2. Charles F. Stanley, *Practicing Basic Spiritual Disciplines* (Nashville: Thomas Nelson, 2009), 17.
3. Burge, "Obedience," 606.

In the Sermon on the Mount, Jesus began with beatitudes that challenged his hearers to attitudes and actions that are humble, mournful, meek, hungry for righteousness, merciful, pure in heart, peacemaking, and prepared to endure persecution with rejoicing (Matt. 5:3–12). These statements are counterintuitive, countercultural, bracing, and inspiring.[4]

Jesus taught that the righteousness of his followers was to exceed that of the scribes and Pharisees (Matt. 5:20). Those religious experts were famously scrupulous about their detailed observance of the law. How would less-knowledgeable disciples of Jesus surpass them in righteousness? They were to grasp the spirit of the law ("You have heard that it was said . . . but I say to you . . .")[5] and apply it, not only to their outward actions but also to the condition of their hearts. That interior examination went beyond the prideful, outward righteousness of the religious leaders.[6]

As Jesus ended his sermon, he emphasized the importance of believers' actions growing out of their belief; there is more to salvation than a profession of faith. "Not everyone who says to me, 'Lord, Lord,' will enter the kingdom of heaven, but only the one who does the will of my Father who is in heaven" (Matt. 7:21).

Dietrich Bonhoeffer, in his classic commentary on Jesus's sermon, declares that obedience is fundamental to belief as well as discipleship. As opposed to a figurative or overly spiritual call, Jesus's call to discipleship "is an actual call . . . because it is only through actual obedience that a man can become liberated to believe."[7] Thus "easy believism" is avoided.[8] Faith is coupled with repentance, and moral and loving action is undertaken, extended even toward one's enemies (Matt. 5:44).

---

4. Michael J. Wilkins, *Matthew*, NIV Application Commentary (Grand Rapids: Zondervan, 2004), 204: "The character of this kingdom life contravenes the values that most people hold dear, because God's blessing rests on the unlikely ones—the poor in spirit, mourners, the meek, the persecuted."

5. See, for example, David L. Turner, *Matthew*, Baker Exegetical Commentary on the New Testament (Grand Rapids: Baker Academic, 2007), 164–65.

6. Grant R. Osborne, *Matthew*, Zondervan Exegetical Commentary on the New Testament 1 (Grand Rapids: Zondervan, 2009), 186–87. Osborne writes that these verses "exemplify the 'better righteousness' Jesus has just demanded, and they further explain how Jesus fulfilled/deepened the law in the new ethics of the kingdom" (introduced in 5:17–20).

7. Bonhoeffer, *Cost of Discipleship*, trans. R. H. Fuller (New York: MacMillan, 1959), 91–92.

8. Bonhoeffer, *Cost of Discipleship*; Gary Collins, *Beyond Easy Believism* (Waco, TX: Word, 1982).

Even Jesus's most condensed ethical exposition, the Sermon on the Mount, is more than mere ethical suggestion. He tells his disciples how to live—in their hearts as well as in their actions. And then he expects them to obey.

The apostle Paul calls his readers to obey, elevating "obedience as one of the constituent parts of faith."[9] For example, in several of Paul's letters he emphasizes theological truths in the earlier portion of the letter and then transitions to ethical implications in the latter portion. Right actions emerge from right ideas. His thinking "combines doctrine with duty, belief with behavior. . . . He integrates creed and conduct. . . . He turns . . . from exposition to exhortation."[10]

In Romans Paul told people how they should live but only after he taught them what they should believe. Because he wanted their actions to be based on sound beliefs, he presented the great truths first, such as the following "famous" ideas: "the gospel . . . is the power of God that brings salvation to everyone who believes" (1:16), and "for all have sinned and fall short of the glory of God, and all are justified freely by his grace through the redemption that came by Christ Jesus" (3:23–24).

After establishing the way he wanted his readers to think in the first eleven chapters,[11] Paul told them how he wanted them to live.[12] Chapters twelve and thirteen are full of ethical exhortations, such as "offer your bodies as a living sacrifice, holy and pleasing to God"[13] (12:1), "hate what is evil; cling to what is good"[14] (12:9), and "let no debt remain outstanding, except the continuing debt to love one another" (13:8). Right actions grow out of right thinking.

---

9. Burge, "Obedience," 606.

10. John Stott, *Romans: God's Good News for the World* (Downers Grove, IL: InterVarsity Press, 1994), 317.

11. After an excursus on how the people of Israel fit into the sovereign plan of God (Rom. 9–11).

12. The "hinge verses" in some of Paul's letters accentuate that actions grow out of faith. Douglas J. Moo says that Romans 12:1–2 has "a pivotal role in Romans." Moo, *The Epistle to the Romans*, New International Commentary on the New Testament (Grand Rapids: Eerdmans, 1996), 748. For other examples of pivotal or hinge verses in Paul's letters, see Ephesians 4:1; Colossians 3:1; and 1 Thessalonians 4:1.

13. "To present" (παραστησαι) is an infinitive, but "the infinitive following Παρακαλω functions as an imperative and should be construed as a command." Thomas R. Schreiner, *Romans*, Baker Exegetical Commentary on the New Testament (Grand Rapids: Baker, 1998), 643.

14. Although these verbs (αποστυγουντες and κολλωμενοι) are both participles, "in the final analysis they function in this same context as imperatives, . . . for it is clear that Paul is giving commands." Schreiner, *Romans*, 664.

Obedience Is Foundational for Relationship

However, the distinguishing factor for a biblical understanding of obedience is not so much the consistent link between hearing and obeying; rather, it is Scripture's call to obey as a component of relationship. "Single-minded obedience grasps the spirit of God's intentions [with his Law] and exceeds God's desires—not with a servant's measured efforts but as people who enjoy a vital and responsive relationship."[15] This biblical obedience-in-relationship idea progresses from the Old Testament understanding of Jewish racial obedience to the law (which Jesus corrected, reframed, and expanded) until it ultimately yields Paul's dual emphasis on both the need for God's people to obey and the assistance promised by God to make that obedience happen.

The Ten Commandments may be the ultimate obedience list, but Walter Brueggemann notes that Israel's obedience to God's commands was intended as a covenantal and relational response. "The oppressive bonds of Egypt are broken [via the exodus]. Now the liberating, covenantal bond of Yahweh is offered."[16]

God revealed himself to Israel in the "awe of theophany" at the Red Sea and at Sinai, but not just to overwhelm them with the realities of his sovereignty. He called them his very own people, pledged to be *their* Sovereign, and offered terms by which their relationship would work for perpetuity. He blessed them by bonding them to himself.

God's commands were nothing short of the intentional, moral component of the relationship. The Decalogue reminded Israel that God is holy (commands one through four); therefore, they should not attempt to use him for their own purposes. Furthermore, Israelites were called to respect their neighbors (commands five through ten). The covenant community "will not degenerate into a society of abuse, disrespect, oppression, and, finally, brutality."[17] These words of relationship between God and humanity defined the quality of Israel's new life.

15. Burge, "Obedience," 606.

16. Walter Brueggemann, *Interpretation and Obedience: From Faithful Reading to Faithful Living* (Minneapolis: Fortress, 1991), 145.

17. Walter Brueggemann, *Subversive Obedience: Truth Telling and the Art of Preaching* (Norwich, UK: SCM, 2011), 58.

Because Yahweh is a different kind of sovereign, Israel is permitted to embrace a very different kind of obedience. This obedience is not an oppressive, despair-inducing obedience, nor is it obedience so rigid and narrow as that of some opponents of Jesus. It is obedience, rather, that is a genuine delight, because it makes humanness possible.[18]

Eugene Peterson identifies this sort of Old Testament understanding of obedience by way of Psalm 132. This psalm "shows obedience as a lively, adventurous response of faith."[19] Grounding the value of obedience in the vows David kept toward God (Ps. 132:2), which resulted in the blessings God gave David (Ps. 132:12–18), Peterson draws on other biblical examples of obedience—and disobedience—to illustrate the value of Scripture's teaching on obedience. The stories provide Christians deeper and broader experience to bolster the need to live lives of obedience. "We need roots in the past to give obedience ballast and breadth."[20]

Furthermore, Old Testament wisdom literature connects faithfulness and morality to the wise. "Faithfulness, judgment, and uprightness are, after all, the characteristics of Yahweh's own person, and are the qualities or stances that Yahweh looks for in people."[21] Throughout the Old Testament, God's people are expected to live and behave consistently in their covenant relationship with him.

In the New Testament, the apostle Paul expanded this understanding of obedience-in-relationship. Building on Jesus's teaching and call, that all who follow him as disciples must obey, Paul made clear that Jesus's disciples have help to obey in the indwelling Spirit of God. This point is particularly clear in the apostle's teaching in the final two chapters in Galatians.

Paul argued that the Galatian Christians had reverted from following the Spirit of God to attempting to fulfill the law by their own merits and energy. "Are you so foolish? Having begun by the Spirit, are you

---

18. Brueggemann, *Interpretation and Obedience*, 145–55.
19. Eugene H. Peterson, *A Long Obedience in the Same Direction: Discipleship in an Instant Society*, 20th anniv. ed. (Downers Grove, IL: InterVarsity Press, 2000), 164. Peterson obtained his evocative title from a quote by Friedrich Nietzsche of all people.
20. Peterson, *Long Obedience*, 170.
21. John Goldingay, *Old Testament Theology*, vol. 2, *Israel's Faith* (Downers Grove, IL: IVP Academic, 2005), 583, in his section on wisdom presenting an ideal.

now being perfected by the flesh?" (Gal. 3:3 ESV). Paul was urging the Galatians (and all Christians by extension) to push forward with a new ethic—a new motivation and a more focused standard of behavior. Obedience is still required but not by means of the tedious, legalistic following of the six hundred-plus commands of the law. Rather, the new ethic is grounded in the Spirit who is not only the source of the Galatians' Christian life but also "their standard of obedience."[22] All the commands can be condensed into one: love (Gal. 5:14). And the Spirit of God will bear that very fruit in the obedient believer (Gal. 5:22–24). Thus "Paul portrays the Christian life under the rubric of 'continuing' or 'walking' in the Spirit, whose chief fruit is love."[23] The remarkable reality that Paul expounds is the ethical context into which a disciple of Jesus has been placed, namely, into the interplay between spiritual empowerment and human obedience. "The power and leading of the Spirit and even the gift of the fruit of the Spirit do not diminish but rather enhance the demand to work and to sow to the Spirit."[24]

Obedience Leads to God's Blessing

But obedience is much more than mimicking good patterns from stories of the past in order to avoid pitfalls experienced by the disobedient. Obedience to the covenant brought the promise of blessing, and disobedience evoked curses (Deut. 27–28). The period of the judges (with its cycles of blessing, disobedience, judgment, cry of pain, and deliverance) illustrates the connection between obedience and God's blessing.[25] The kings of Israel and Judah either "did evil in the eyes of the LORD" (Jehoram; 2 Kings 8:18) or "did what was good and right in the eyes of the LORD his God (Asa; 2 Chron. 14:2)," and Yahweh took note and responded.[26] The prophets excoriated Israel and Judah for their

---

22. John M. G. Barclay, *Obeying the Truth: Paul's Ethics in Galatians* (Minneapolis: Fortress, 1991), 155.

23. Barclay, *Obeying the Truth*, 223.

24. Barclay, *Obeying the Truth*, 226.

25. See, for example, Daniel I. Block, *Judges, Ruth*, New American Commentary 6 (Nashville: B&H, 1999), 58.

26. John Goldingay, *Old Testament Theology*, vol. 1, *Israel's Gospel* (Downers Grove, IL: IVP Academic, 2003), 632–42 chronicled Yahweh's reactions under the sub-headings anger, continuing commitment, rejection tempered by grace, pity, long-temperedness, and mercy that eventually runs out.

unfaithfulness and disobedience, lamenting that God's people failed to live up to the calling and privilege of the covenant.[27]

What makes those stories valuable is noting that the obedient people experienced God's blessings because they had a relationship with him. Even as a good understanding of the biblical past provides "ballast and breadth" to obedience, "we need a vision of the future to give obedience direction and goal."[28] This full understanding of obedience does not discount stories like that of Job, who faithfully obeyed but whose blessings were spoiled and not restored until after he endured deep sorrow and difficulty. Nevertheless, even Job's story illustrates that "obedience is not a stodgy plodding in the ruts of religion, it is a hopeful race toward God's promises."[29]

After washing their feet and reminding them of their new roles of servants and messengers, Jesus exhorted the apostles, "Now that you know these things, you will be blessed if you do them" (John 13:17). When a woman in his audience blurted out what a blessing it would have been to have borne and nursed him, Jesus retorted, "Blessed rather are those who hear the word of God and obey it" (Luke 11:28). This was a reiteration of his prioritization of obedient disciples over his own flesh and blood, as he had earlier declared, "My mother and brothers are those who hear God's word and put it into practice" (Luke 8:21).

The blessing of sanctification is the spiritual process by which sinners saved by grace become more holy. It is the unstoppable work of God in our lives. Paul was "confident of this, that he who began a good work in you will carry it on to completion until the day of Christ Jesus" (Phil. 1:6). God will continue his work of redemption until the day of Jesus Christ. At the end of 1 Thessalonians, Paul offered this prayer: "May God himself, the God of peace, sanctify you through and through. May your whole spirit, soul and body be kept blameless at the coming of our Lord Jesus Christ. The one who calls you is faithful, and he will do it" (5:23–24). Because he is confident in God's faithfulness, Paul is sure that what he wishes and prays for will happen.

---

27. See Goldingay, *Old Testament Theology*, 2:254–349. See especially his chapter, "The Nightmare," which details the problem of continuing sin among the covenant people of God and its consequences.

28. Peterson, *Long Obedience*, 170.

29. Peterson, *Long Obedience*, 168.

Not only did Paul teach and promise that God would sanctify us, but he also commanded believers regarding their spiritual growth and moral character development. Such commands include "train yourself to be godly" (1 Tim. 4:7), "rid yourselves of all such things as these: anger, rage, malice, slander, and filthy language from your lips" (Col. 3:8), and "stand firm. Let nothing move you. Always give yourselves fully to the work of the Lord, because you know that your labor in the Lord is not in vain" (1 Cor. 15:58). Thus the apostle called and commanded disciples to exert effort toward sanctification, practicing what he preached with tenacious consistency. "Join together in following my example, brothers and sisters, and just as you have us as a model, keep your eyes on those who live as we do" (Phil. 3:17). All believers—and certainly ministry leaders—must obey this command of the apostle and imitate him as he imitated Christ (1 Cor. 11:1). By doing so, we will join the chain of those who serve as worthy examples to others.

God's work of salvation and call to serve him include life transformation that is evident in obvious and practical ways. Our character, speech, and actions must align with our professed faith. That is the purpose of grace. In Titus 2:11–14, Paul wrote,

> For the grace of God has appeared that offers salvation to all people. It teaches us to say "No" to ungodliness and worldly passions, and to live self-controlled, upright and godly lives in this present age, while we wait for the blessed hope—the appearing of the glory of our great God and Savior, Jesus Christ, who gave himself for us to redeem us from all wickedness and to purify for himself a people that are his very own, eager to do what is good.

Obedience Defines Success

In *One Small Barking Dog: How to Live a Life That's Hard to Ignore*, Ed Gungor writes:

> [Georges] Seurat is considered the father of pointillism, a form of art in which images are painted using tiny dots of color. Seurat's paintings are amazing to behold because, from a distance, they appear as slices of life at the park, the harbor, the opera, the circus,

the beach, or in a field. But up close they're really just a collection of thousands of teeny, tiny dots—literally infinitesimal specks of color. It's only when one steps back for a more objective look that the "big picture" is revealed.

I believe this is how God works his will in our world. He uses millions of teeny tiny dabs of obedience from the ordinary lives of believers to bring about the big picture—his dream for the world.[30]

One dot—what difference could one little dot make? For King Saul, one point of disobedience tainted everything. When confronted by the prophet, he argued that his dot of disobedience was inconsequential because he intended to sacrifice the lambs he hadn't destroyed obediently. Samuel let him know that God did not delight in his ill-gotten sacrifice but wanted his obedience (1 Sam. 15:22). Imagine what thoughts the original recipients of this book had when they reflected on the juxtaposition between sacrifice and obedience. They were in captivity without a temple or an altar for sacrifice, but they could still be obedient—the service in which God really delights.

One dot—what difference could one little dot make? For Moses, one point of disobedience tainted everything: striking the rock at Meribah. Because of his disobedience, he was not allowed to lead the children of Israel into the promised land.

While one dot can make a difference, as it did in King Saul's or Moses's case, another question is worth exploring: What difference can a lifetime of dots make? One act of obedience here and another act of obedience there become a portrait of a beautiful life.

With the reflection loop, you intentionally close the gap between your understanding of God's truth and your behavior. In other words, you are working on being obedient to what God demands of you for your life and ministry.

One way to define success in ministry is by living a life of obedience to God. Another is to be a faithful servant who lives up to your potential.

---

30. Ed Gungor, *One Small Barking Dog: How to Live a Life That's Hard to Ignore* (New York: Howard, 2010), 72–73.

FAITHFULNESS AND ACHIEVING YOUR POTENTIAL IN MINISTRY

In the parable of the talents, the master entrusts different sums of money to three servants before embarking on a long journey. Upon his return, the master calls them to account for their stewardship. The first two servants report a 100 percent gain and are equally commended, entrusted with proportionate additional responsibility, and rewarded. The third servant reports that he hid the treasure and then returned it to the master. This servant excuses his behavior by impugning the character of the master. The master harshly rebukes him, divests him of the money in trust, and punishes him harshly.

The parable of the talents is part of the eschatological discourse of Jesus in Matthew 24–25. The master in the parable corresponds to Christ, and the master's long journey and return correspond to Christ's physical absence from earth and second coming. Most important, the settling of accounts and the servants' consequences correspond to the final judgment. This can be called a "readiness parable" because it considers how one can be ready for the return of Christ and his final judgment.[31]

So how can one be ready for the final accounting? According to R. T. France, "This parable calls followers of Jesus to responsible activity—or, in the imagery of the parable itself, to maximize one's potential for the benefit of the kingdom of God."[32] "To be 'ready' for the master's return means to use the intervening time to maximum profit."[33]

Scholars commonly agree that the essential point of emphasis in this parable is accountable, faithful stewardship on the part of believers for God's purposes. Klyne Snodgrass writes, "The parable is about stewardship" and "is a call to faithfulness and a warning against unfaithfulness."[34]

---

31. Richard T. France, "On Being Ready (Matthew 25:1–46)," in *The Challenge of the Parables*, ed. Richard N. Longenecker (Grand Rapids: Eerdmans, 2000), 177–95. Cf. Michael J. Wilkins, *Matthew*, 799, 814–15; Nolland, *Matthew*, 1012, 1020; and Osborne, *Matthew*, 920.

32. France, "On Being Ready," 189.

33. R. T. France, *The Gospel of Matthew*, International Commentary on the New Testament (Grand Rapids: Eerdmans, 2007), 951.

34. Klyne Snodgrass, *Stories with Intent: A Comprehensive Guide to the Parables of Jesus* (Grand Rapids: Eerdmans, 2008), 533–34. Although Craig L. Blomberg, *Interpreting the Parables* (Downers Grove, IL: InterVarsity Press, 1990), 214, identifies three points to this parable, they all relate to accountable stewardship that results in polarized outcomes.

Arland Hultgren says, "The accent is upon the disciple's being faithful in his or her use of the gift given, regardless of how much has been entrusted."[35] Likewise, Brad Young deduces that "the underlying theme of the parable of the Talents . . . is stewardship."[36] "The ultimate concern of the story is the faithful stewardship of God's gracious gifts."[37]

What Are Talents?

In the parable, talents are entrusted to the servants—five to the first, two to another, one to a third. A talent was a unit of wealth in New Testament times equal to 6,000 denarii. Since a denarius was the value of a common laborer's daily wage, a talent would correspond to about twenty years' wages (much more than the NIV's note of "more than a thousand dollars").[38] These enormous sums help to emphasize the trust placed in the servants and the responsibility laid upon them. By application we are to understand that God has been extremely generous in his bestowal of gifts to us for kingdom purposes, and we should anticipate his keen interest in our stewardship of them.

The confusion modern English readers have about the word *talents* in the parable is rooted in the etymology of the English word *talent*, which can be traced back to this very parable.[39] However, as we apply the parable to our lives, we should see that the gift we've been given is neither limited to wealth nor identical to our modern conception of talents. God's gifts are more comprehensive and dovetail with a holistic view of stewardship. All that we are and all that we have are from God and intended by him to be used for his glory.

Ministers should reckon that the gifts they steward include the grace-gift of their ministries (Acts 20:24; Rom. 1:5; 15:15–16; 1 Cor. 3:10;

---

35. Arland J. Hultgren, *The Parables of Jesus: A Commentary*, Bible in Its World (Grand Rapids: Eerdmans, 2000), 278.

36. Brad H. Young, *The Parables: Jewish Tradition and Christian Interpretation* (Peabody, MA: Hendrickson, 1998), 82.

37. Young, *Parables*, 85. See also Osborne, *Matthew*, 920.

38. Snodgrass, *Stories with Intent*, 66, 528; Hultgren, *Parables of Jesus*, 274–75; D. A. Carson, *Matthew*, in *Matthew-Mark*, Expositor's Bible Commentary 9, rev. ed. (Grand Rapids: Zondervan, 2010), 579. Thus, the first servant was entrusted with wealth roughly equal to 100 years of earnings for a common laborer. Nolland comments that "five talents . . . would have employed a hundred day labourers for about a year" (Nolland, *Matthew*, 1014).

39. Snodgrass, *Stories with Intent*, 528; Hultgren, *Parables of Jesus*, 275.

Gal. 1:15–16; Eph. 3:2; 6–7), the message of the gospel (Acts 20:24; 1 Cor. 4:1–2; 15:3–4; 2 Cor. 5:18–20; Gal. 1:11–12), the gifts of the Holy Spirit (Rom. 12:6; 1 Cor. 12:11; 1 Pet. 4:10), and adequacy for ministry bestowed by the power of God (1 Cor. 15:10; 2 Cor. 3:4–6; Eph. 6:10; Col. 1:28–29; 2 Tim. 2:1).

Two Servants Were Faithful

In the parable of the talents, the first two servants are faithful and fruitful and therefore receive commendations and rewards. These characters in the story are worthy of our emulation:[40] we want to be like them, do likewise, and garner a similar response from our Master one day. These two servants are entrusted with enormous but different sums, "each according to his ability" (Matt. 25:15).[41] Both servants engage in their master's business on his behalf with the gifts entrusted to them for that purpose, and both are equally fruitful in proportion to their trust. In response to their fruitful stewardship, both are commended exactly the same way: "Well done, good and faithful servant!" (Matt. 25:21, 23). The master commends their character ("good") as well as their behavior ("faithful"). The latter springs from the former just as authentic faith issues forth in good works (James 2:18). Modern believers often express their hope that Jesus will on that day say to them, "Well done, good and faithful servant" (Matt. 25:21, 23)! This is a holy aspiration inspired by this parable. Jesus must be pleased that so many identify with these servants as he intended we would. The further statement, "enter into the joy of your master" (25:21, 23 ESV), alludes to eschatological ecstasy. In the context of the apocalyptic discourse of Matthew 24–25, we are intended to understand this to correspond to our glorious hope of being welcomed into the beatific, eternal presence of God.[42]

---

40. Leland Ryken summarizes how "storytellers (including those in the Bible) achieve their persuasive end by controlling our patterns of sympathy and aversion (or antipathy) to individual pieces of characterization and ultimately to an entire character." Ryken, *How Bible Stories Work: A Guided Study of Narrative Literature*, Reading the Bible as Literature (Wooster, OH: Weaver, 2015), 46–47.

41. There is neither gloating by the first servant nor grumbling by the second over the variance in their abilities and degrees of responsibility. Some are more gifted by God than others, but whatever our degree of giftedness and responsibility, we are to humbly receive it and get busy employing it for the Master's purposes. Cf. France, *Matthew*, 953–54.

42. Joachim Jeremias believes the word for joy here (*chara*) should be understood to

Two Servants Reached Their Potential

There is repetition in the accounts of the first two servants—proportionate investment returns, identical commendations, rewards, and further responsibilities. Both reached their potential and pleased their master with the return they earned. Nolland comments that "a rhythm has begun to develop, which creates an expectation as to how things should be in the third case."[43] When the account of the third servant breaks the rhythm, we take particular interest and anticipate an important lesson, especially since his outcome is left until the end of the story.[44]

The third servant is entrusted with the least wealth, and in fear he buries it rather than investing it. When the day of reckoning comes, he returns exactly what had been entrusted to him. Some suggest the storytelling technique of "reversal" is at work here. Burying treasure was not uncommon in the first-century world. In fact, Jesus himself alludes to the practice without judgment (Matt. 13:44). Joachim Jeremias notes, "Burying (Matt. 25.18), according to rabbinical law, was regarded as the best security against theft. Anyone who buried a pledge or a deposit immediately upon receipt of it, was free from liability."[45] So Jesus's listeners may have expected this treasure burier to be commended. Jesus reverses that expectation by revealing the devastating rebuke and punishment the third servant receives.[46]

Why is the third servant maligned? First, although he was not explicitly charged to invest the treasure, we come to learn that investment was the master's intent. Even if we feel some sympathy for the third servant

mean "feast," so that this statement resonates with the messianic banquet. Jeremias, *The Parables of Jesus*, 2nd ed. (New York: Scribner's, 1972), 60n42, Cf. Osborne, *Matthew*, 925.

43. Nolland, *Matthew*, 1015.

44. Snodgrass, *Stories with Intent*, 19–20, explains that parables are often characterized by a focus on the end of the story and exhorted interpreters to *"pay particular attention to the rule of end stress"* (30). Cf. Leland Ryken, *Jesus the Hero: A Guided Literary Study of the Gospels*, Reading the Bible as Literature (Wooster, OH: Weaver, 2016), 99. C. H. Dodd applies this rule to this parable: "It is surely evident that the central interest lies in the scene of the reckoning and in particular in the position of the cautious servant. . . . The details of the story are subordinate to this dramatic climax. . . . All is contrived to throw into strong relief the character of the scrupulous servant who will take no risks." Dodd, *The Parables of the Kingdom* (New York: Scribner's, 1961), 118.

45. Jeremias, *Parables*, 61n51.

46. Blomberg says, "Jesus's condemnation of the man who hid his master's money may thus have caused strong shockwaves." He also deems this parable to have "a tragic plot—the lesson to be derived from the evil servant is the dominant one" (Blomberg, *Interpreting the Parables*, 214–15).

due to a lack of explicit direction regarding investment, we still learn the same lesson from Jesus in his telling of the story: in Jesus we have a spiritual leader who expects risk-taking for his cause. And as the master in the story implies, the third servant's own words condemn him (Matt. 25:26).[47] Rather than expressing respect to the master as he returned what was his, he denigrates his master's character in their accounting interview. He claims to know that the master is "a hard man, harvesting where you have not sown and gathering where you have not scattered seed" (Matt. 25:24). Are we to believe that this description of the master in the story has some parallel to God in application? We have no such obligation. As an unfaithful steward, the third servant should also be seen as an untrustworthy witness.[48]

Whereas the first two servants were commended both for their character ("good") and behavior ("faithful"), the third servant is castigated for his character ("wicked") and his behavior ("lazy"). Earnest hearers and readers of this story will take the warning and encouragement intended. We should not hoard the gifts we received from God and shirk our responsibility; we must employ them for the master's benefit.[49] Doing so will bring us lasting benefit and will stave off the utter ruin that awaits if we are wickedly lazy.

Faithfulness and Reaching Your Potential Define Success

Success in ministry cannot be calculated by comparing your ministerial statistics with those of other ministers. We came of age in ministry as pastors during the peak of the church growth movement's influence. While the leaders of the movement never intimated that obedience and

---

47. Carson, *Matthew*, 581. In contrast, Hultgren, *Parables of Jesus*, 276, misses the storyteller's intent when he writes that "the master admits that he is known to be ruthless and rapacious in business." We need not concede that the master stipulates to that. He is only using the wicked servant's errant judgment against him.

48. See, for example, Wilkins, *Matthew*, 820; and Young, *Parables*, 95: "The failure was based upon a misunderstanding of the divine nature." In contrast, Nolland entertains the possibility that we are to see some truth in this image of God as "one who is ultimately dominant. God asserts his claim to be Lord of all and will ultimately make good that claim" (Nolland, *Matthew*, 1019). France agrees there is some valid point to this characterization of God: "Even if God is not unreasonable and exploitative, the parable as a whole emphasizes that he makes exacting demands on his people. He is not to be fobbed off with a lame excuse" (France, *Matthew*, 956).

49. Carson, *Matthew*, 581.

faithfulness were unimportant, the focus of the movement was for pastors to produce numerical results, including but not limited to expanding the physical footprint of the church building, raising bigger budgets, and increasing attendance in the worship service. So during the formative years of our ministries, we heard the message loud and clear: good pastors lead their churches to grow.

And the truth is . . . some do. Some of the churches we have served grew and received recognition from the denomination for their growth. But those statistics are no substitute for obedience, faithfulness, and reaching our potential in ministry.

False Dichotomy

Does it need to be one or the other? While statistical success is no substitute for intangible measurements like obedience, faithfulness, and reaching our potential in ministry, numerical measurements are still important.

People are important. Numbers are not. But when the numbers represent changed lives, then they are important. They are not just numbers anymore. They represent people. Comparing your numerical results to other people's results is not healthy, but monitoring your results in proportion to your potential is. The two servants who were rewarded were faithful. They reached their potential, and they got results—both doubled what their master gave them.

Success is not a singular destination. It is not a single point of light to set our eyes on. Instead, it is more like a constellation of stars. Meeting growth covenant goals or ministry goals is one star in the constellation of success, but there are many others. Baptisms, budgets, and buildings could be part of the constellation, just never all of the constellation. Approval of mentors, recognition from peers, and the gratitude of those we serve are also indicators of success. Obedience, faithfulness, and reaching our potential are definitely important indicators.

Our ministry success will not be determined by authors of a textbook, mentors, peer groups, or professors. Our success is determined by the Lord, who alone is worthy to say, "Well done, good and faithful servant!" (Matt. 25:23).

Our sincere prayer is that you will one day hear those words.

BIBLIOGRAPHY

Adams, Kathleen. "The Development of Journal Writing for Well-Being." *The Illustrated Encyclopedia of Mind-Body Medicine*. The Rosen Group, 1999. https://journaltherapy.com/get-training/short-program-journal-to-the-self/journal-to-the-self/journal-writing-history/.

Augustine. *Christian Doctrine*. In *St. Augustin's City of God and Christian Doctrine*. Edited by Philip Schaff. Translated by J. F. Shaw. Vol. 2 of *A Select Library of the Nicene and Post-Nicene Fathers of the Christian Church*. Buffalo, NY: Christian Literature Company, 1887.

Ballard, Paul. "The Bible in Theological Reflection: Indication of the History of Scripture." *Practical Theology* 4, no. 1 (2011). http://ezproxy.ccu.edu:2082/ehost/pdfviewer /pdfviewer?vid=5&sid=2c994843–1480–4bd0–8361 –388400e7ba79%40sessionmgr4008.

———. "Reflections on Theological Reflection." *Modern Believing* 40, no. 3 (July 1999). http://ezproxy.ccu.edu:2082/ehost/pdfviewer/pdfviewer?vid=4&sid= dcfd2914–3c32–4a08-bcb6–1c959187c1a3%40sessionmgr4006.

———. "Theological Reflection and Providence." *Practical Theology* 1, no. 3 (2009). http://ezproxy.ccu.edu:2082/ehost/pdfviewer/pdfviewer?vid=3&sid=0d2a 2552–2d34–4744–9e69–3349eb59479e%40sessionmgr4007.

Barclay, John M. G. *Obeying the Truth: Paul's Ethics in Galatians*. Minneapolis: Fortress, 1991.

Barker, Eric. "5 Science-Backed Ways to Break Your Phone Addiction." *The Week*, March 29, 2017. http://theweek.com/articles/688639/5-sciencebacked-ways -break-phone-addiction.

Bauckham, Richard. *Jesus and the Eyewitnesses: The Gospels as Eyewitness Testimony*. Grand Rapids: Eerdmans, 2006.

Bird, Michael. *Evangelical Theology: A Biblical and Systematic Introduction*. Grand Rapids: Zondervan, 2013.

Block, Daniel I. *Judges, Ruth*. The New American Commentary 6. Nashville: B&H, 1999.

Blomberg, Craig L. *Interpreting the Parables*. Downers Grove, IL: IVP Academic, 1990.

Bock, Darrell L. *Luke 1:1–9:50*. Baker Exegetical Commentary on the New Testament. Grand Rapids: Baker, 1994.

————. *Luke 9:51–24:53*. Baker Exegetical Commentary on the New Testament. Grand Rapids: Baker, 1996.

Bolsinger, Tod. *Canoeing the Mountains: Christian Leadership in Uncharted Territory*. Downers Grove, IL: IVP Books, 2015.

Bonhoeffer, Dietrich. *The Cost of Discipleship*. Translated by R. H. Fuller. New York: MacMillan, 1959.

Brock, Brian. *Singing the Ethos of God: On the Place of Christian Ethics in Scripture*. Grand Rapids: Eerdmans, 2007.

Brueggemann, Walter. *The Bible Makes Sense*. Louisville: Westminster John Knox, 2001.

————. *Interpretation and Obedience: From Faithful Reading to Faithful Living*. Minneapolis: Fortress, 1991.

————. *Subversive Obedience: Truth Telling and the Art of Preaching*. Norwich, UK: SCM, 2011.

Burridge, Richard A. *Imitating Jesus: An Inclusive Approach to New Testament Ethics*. Grand Rapids: Eerdmans, 2007.

Carson, D. A. *Matthew*. In *Matthew-Mark*, Expositor's Bible Commentary 9. Revised edition. Grand Rapids: Zondervan, 2010.

————. *The Sermon on the Mount: An Exegetical Exposition of Matthew 5–7*. Grand Rapids: Baker Books, 1978.

Chechowich, Faye. "Journaling as a Spiritual Discipline." Bible Gateway. https://www.biblegateway.com/resources/scripture-engagement/journaling-scripture/spiritual-discipline.

Cloud, Henry. *Boundaries for Leaders: Results, Relationships, and Being Ridiculously in Charge*. New York: HarperBusiness, 2013.

Collins, Gary R. *Beyond Easy Believism*. Waco: Word, 1982.

Covey, Stephen R. *The 7 Habits of Highly Effective People*. Coral Gables, FL: Mango, 2017. Kindle edition.

Culpepper, R. Alan. *Anatomy of the Fourth Gospel: A Study in Literary Design*. Philadelphia: Fortress, 1983.

Dodd, C. H. *The Parables of the Kingdom*. New York: Scribner's, 1961.

Drucker, Peter F. *The Executive in Action*. New York: Harper Business, 1996.

Ebstyne King, Pamela, and James L. Furrow. "Religion as a Resource for Positive Youth Development: Religion, Social Capital, and Moral Outcomes." *Developmental Psychology* 40, no. 5 (2004): 703–13.

Erickson, Millard J. *Christian Theology*. 3rd ed. Grand Rapids: Baker Academic, 2013.

Fee, Gordon D. *Philippians*. IVP New Testament Commentary 11. Downers Grove, IL: IVP Academic, 1999.

Floding, Matthew, ed. *Welcome to Theological Field Education*. Herndon, NC: Alban Institute, 2011.

Foley, Edward. "Reflective Believing: Reimagining Theological Reflection in an Age of Diversity." *Reflective Practice: Formation and Supervision in Ministry* 34 (2014): 60–75.

France, R. T. *The Gospel of Mark: A Commentary on the Greek Text*. New International Greek Testament Commentary. Grand Rapids: Eerdmans, 2002.

———. *The Gospel of Matthew*. New International Commentary on the New Testament. Grand Rapids: Eerdmans, 2007.

———. "On Being Ready" (Matthew 25:1–46). In *The Challenge of the Parables*, edited by Richard N. Longenecker. Grand Rapids: Eerdmans, 2000.

Freire, Paulo. *Pedagogy of the Oppressed*. 30th anniv. ed. Translated by Myra Bergman Ramos. New York: Continuum International, 2000.

Garrett, James Leo, Jr. *Systematic Theology: Biblical, Historical, and Evangelical*. Vol. 2. 2nd ed. Eugene, OR: Wipf & Stock, 2014.

Gill, David W. *Becoming Good: Building Moral Character*. Downers Grove, IL: IVP Books, 2009.

Goldingay, John. *Old Testament Theology*. 2 vols. Downers Grove, IL: IVP Academic, 2003–5.

Graham, Elaine, Heather Walton, and Frances Ward. *Theological Reflection: Methods*. London: SCM, 2005.

Green, Joel B. *The Gospel of Luke*. New International Commentary on the New Testament. Grand Rapids: Eerdmans, 1997.

Grenz, Stanley J. *Theology for the Community of God*. Grand Rapids: Eerdmans, 2000.

Grudem, Wayne. *Systematic Theology: An Introduction to Biblical Doctrine*. Grand Rapids: Zondervan, 2000.

Gungor, Ed. *One Small Barking Dog: How to Live a Life That's Hard to Ignore*. New York: Howard, 2010.

Hart, Trevor. *Faith Thinking: The Dynamics of Christian Theology*. Eugene, OR: Wipf & Stock, 1995.

Heifitz, Ronald A., Marty Linsky, and Alexander Grashow. *The Practice of Adaptive Leadership: Tools and Tactics for Changing Your Organization and the World*. Boston: Harvard Business Publishing, 2009.

Hillman, George M., Jr. *Ministry Greenhouse: Cultivating Environments for Practical Learning*. Herndon, NC: Alban Institute, 2008.

———, ed. *Preparing for Ministry: A Practical Guide to Theological Field Education*. Grand Rapids: Kregel, 2008.

Hollinger, Dennis. *Choosing the Good: Christian Ethics in a Complex World*. Grand Rapids: Baker Academic, 2002.

Hultgren, Arland J. *The Parables of Jesus: A Commentary*. The Bible in Its World. Grand Rapids: Eerdmans, 2000.

Humphreys, Fisher. *Thinking about God*. 2nd ed. New Orleans: Insight, 1994.

Iorg, Jeff. *Is God Calling Me? Answering the Question Every Leader Asks*. Nashville: B&H, 2008.

Jeremias, Joachim. *The Parables of Jesus*. 2nd rev. ed. New York: Charles Scribner's Sons, 1972.

Jobes, Karen H. *1 Peter*. Baker Exegetical Commentary on the New Testament. Grand Rapids: Baker Academic, 2005.

Keener, Craig S. *The Gospel of John: A Commentary.* Vol. 1. Peabody, MA: Hendrickson, 2003.

———. *The Gospel of Matthew: A Socio-Rhetorical Commentary.* Grand Rapids: Eerdmans, 2009.

Kernaghan, Ronald J. *Mark.* IVP New Testament Commentary. Downers Grove, IL: IVP Academic, 2007.

Kidner, Derek. *Proverbs.* Tyndale Old Testament Commentaries. Downers Grove, IL: IVP Academic, 1964.

Killen, Patricia O'Connell, and John de Beer. *The Art of Theological Reflection.* New York: Crossroad, 1994.

Kinast, Robert L. *Let Ministry Teach: A Guide to Theological Reflection.* Collegeville, MN: Liturgical, 1996.

Kittel, Gerhard, ed. *Theological Dictionary of the New Testament.* Vol. 4. Translated and edited by Geoffrey W. Bromiley. Grand Rapids: Eerdmans, 1967.

Laney, Marti Olsen. *The Introvert Advantage: How Quiet People Can Thrive in an Extrovert World.* New York: Workman, 2002.

Lepsinger, Richard, and Anntoinette D. Luicia. *The Art and Science of 360° Feedback.* San Francisco: Jossey-Bass, 1997.

Lewis, C. S. *The Weight of Glory and Other Addresses.* Grand Rapids: Eerdmans, 1949.

Longenecker, Richard N. *The Epistle to the Romans.* New International Greek Testament Commentary. Grand Rapids: Eerdmans, 2016.

MacDonald, Gordon, and Gail MacDonald. "Restoring Your Soul." In *Refresh, Renew, Revive,* edited by H. B. London Jr. Colorado Springs: Focus on the Family Publishing, 1996.

Martin, Jim. "Journaling as a Spiritual Discipline." *Leaven* 2, no. 4, art. 8 (1992). http://digitalcommons.pepperdine.edu/leaven/vol2/iss4/8.

Maston, T. B. *Biblical Ethics: A Guide to the Ethical Message of the Scripture from Genesis through Revelation.* Macon, GA: Mercer University Press, 1997.

McCarty, Doran C. "Theological Reflection." In *The Supervised Ministry.* Mill Valley, CA: Golden Gate Baptist Theological Seminary, 1982.

Michaels, J. Ramsey. *The Gospel of John.* New International Commentary on the New Testament. Grand Rapids: Eerdmans, 2010.

Migliore, Daniel L. *Faith Seeking Understanding: An Introduction to Christian Theology.* 2nd ed. Grand Rapids: Eerdmans, 2004.

Moo, Douglas J. *The Epistle to the Romans.* New International Commentary on the New Testament. Grand Rapids: Eerdmans, 1996.

Mulholland, Robert, and Ruth Haley Barton. *Invitation to a Journey: A Roadmap for Spiritual Formation.* Exp. ed. Downers Grove, IL: IVP Books, 2016.

Myers, Isabel B. *MBTI Manual: A Guide to the Development and Use of the Myers-Briggs Type Indicator.* 3rd ed. Palo Alto, CA: Consulting Psychologists, 1998.

Nolland, John. *The Gospel of Matthew: A Commentary on the Greek Text.* New International Greek Testament Commentary. Grand Rapids: Eerdmans, 2005.

Osborne, Grant R. *Matthew.* Zondervan Exegetical Commentary on the New Testament. Grand Rapids: Zondervan, 2010.

Osmer, Richard R. *Practical Theology: An Introduction.* Grand Rapids: Eerdmans, 2008.

Paton, John. "Some Reflections on Theological Reflection." *The Journal of Christian Ministry* 2 (2010): 1–23.

Peterson, Eugene H. *A Long Obedience in the Same Direction: Discipleship in an Instant Society.* 20th anniv. ed. Downers Grove, IL: IVP Books, 2000.

Poling, James, and Donald Miller. *Foundations for a Practical Theology of Ministry.* Nashville: Abingdon, 1985.

Progoff, Ira. *At a Journal Workshop: Writing to Access the Power of the Unconscious and Evoke Creative Ability.* Beachwood, OH: Dialogue House Library, 1975.

Pyle, William T., and Mary Alice Seals, eds. *Experiencing Ministry Supervision: A Field-Based Approach.* Nashville: B&H Academic, 1995.

Reid, Steven. "Carleton Study finds People Spending a Third of Job Time on Email." Carleton Newsroom, April 20, 2017. https://newsroom.carleton.ca/archives/2017/04/20/carleton-study-finds-people-spending-third-job-time-email/.

Renovaré Team. "Prayer Journaling: Styles and Examples." Renovaré, February 1, 2017, https://renovare.org/articles/prayer-journaling-styles-examples.

Reuschling, Wyndy Corbin. *Reviving Evangelical Ethics: The Promises and Pitfalls of Classic Models of Morality.* Grand Rapids: Brazos, 2008.

Richter, Jean Paul. Preface to *The Notebooks of Leonardo DaVinci.* By Leonardo Da Vinci. Vol. 1. Translated by Jean Paul Richter (1888; Project Gutenberg, 2004), http://www.gutenberg.org /files/4998/4998-8.txt.

Rowell, Ed. *Go the Distance: 21 Habits and Attitudes for Winning at Life.* Nashville: B&H, 2002.

Ryken, Leland. *How Bible Stories Work: A Guided Study of Narrative Literature.* Reading the Bible as Literature. Wooster, OH: Weaver, 2015.

———. *Jesus the Hero: A Guided Literary Study of the Gospels.* Reading the Bible as Literature. Wooster, OH: Weaver, 2016.

Schreiner, Thomas R. *Paul, Apostle of God's Glory in Christ: A Pauline Theology.* Downers Grove, IL: IVP Academic, 2001.

———. *Romans.* Baker Exegetical Commentary on the New Testament. Grand Rapids: Baker Academic, 1998.

Segundo, Juan-Luis. *The Liberation of Theology.* New York: Orbis, 1976.

Shōnagon, Sei. *The Pillow Book.* Translated by Meredith McKinney. London: Penguin, 2007.

Smedes, Lewis. *Mere Morality: What God Expects from Ordinary People.* Grand Rapids: Eerdmans, 1989.

Smith, Christian. "Theorizing Religious Effects among American Adolescents." *Journal for the Scientific Study of Religion* 42, no. 1 (2003): 17–30.

Snodgrass, Klyne. *Ephesians.* NIV Application Commentary. Grand Rapids: Zondervan, 1996.

————. *Stories with Intent: A Comprehensive Guide to the Parables of Jesus*. Grand Rapids: Eerdmans, 2008.

Stanley, Charles F. *Practicing Basic Spiritual Disciplines*. Nashville: Thomas Nelson, 2009.

Stone, Howard W., and James O. Duke. *How to Think Theologically*. 3rd ed. Minneapolis: Fortress, 2013.

Stott, John. *Romans: God's Good News for the World*. Bible Speaks Today. Downers Grove, IL: IVP Academic, 1994.

Swenson, Richard A. *Margin: Restoring Emotional, Physical, Financial, and Time Reserves to Overloaded Lives*. Colorado Springs: NavPress, 2004.

Swetland, Kenneth L. Lecture. Evangelical Association of Theological Field Educators. Gordon-Conwell Theological Seminary. Hamilton, MA. 2012.

Treier, Daniel J., ed. *Evangelical Dictionary of Theology*. 3rd ed. Grand Rapids: Baker Academic, 2017.

Tripp, Paul David. *Dangerous Calling: Confronting the Unique Challenges of Pastoral Ministry*. Wheaton, IL: Crossway, 2012.

Trull, Joe E., and R. Robert Creech. *Ethics for Christian Ministry: Moral Formation for 21st-Century Leaders*. Grand Rapids: Baker Academic, 2017.

Trull, Joe. *Walking in the Way: An Introduction to Christian Ethics*. Nashville: B&H, 1997.

Turlejska, E., and M. A. Baker. "Aspirin Enhances Evaporation in Hydrated and Dehydrated Rats." *Canadian Journal of Physiology and Pharmacology* 66, no. 1 (January 1988): 72–76. https://www.ncbi.nlm.nih.gov/pubmed/3370538.

Turner, David L. *Matthew*. Baker Exegetical Commentary on the New Testament. Grand Rapids: Baker Academic, 2007.

Volf, Miroslav. *Captive to the Word of God: Engaging the Scriptures for Contemporary Theological Reflection*. Grand Rapids: Eerdmans, 2010.

Ward, Pete. *Introducing Practical Theology*. Grand Rapids: Baker Academic, 2017.

Warren, Rick. "What I Learned from Billy." *Christianity Today*, February 21, 2018. https://www.christianitytoday.com/ct/2018/billy-graham/rick-warren-what-i-learned-from-billy-graham.html.

Whitehead, James D., and Evelyn Eaton Whitehead. *Method in Ministry: Theological Reflection and Christian Ministry*. New York: Seabury, 1980.

Wilkins, Michael J. *Matthew*. NIV Application Commentary. Grand Rapids: Zondervan, 2004.

Williams, Dennis E. "Church Staff Relations." In *Preparing for Christian Ministry: An Evangelical Approach*, edited by David P. Gushee and Walter C. Jackson. Grand Rapids: Baker, 1996.

Williams, Rowan. *On Christian Theology*. Oxford: Wiley-Blackwell, 2000.

Wilson, Jim L. *Pastoral Ministry in the Real World: Loving, Teaching, and Leading God's People*. 2nd ed. Bellingham, WA: Lexham, 2018.

Young, Brad H. *The Parables: Jewish Tradition and Christian Interpretation*. Peabody, MA: Hendrickson, 1998.

SCRIPTURE INDEX

GENERAL INDEX